Meant for More
A Testimony of Faith

Meant for More
A Testimony of Faith

Written by
Victoria Belcastro-Ray

Published in the United States of America

ISBN 978-1-962110-60-0 (SC)

Library of Congress Control Number: 2024924278

Victoria Belcastro-Ray Books
222 West 6th Street
Suite 400, San Pedro, CA, 90731
www.stellarliterary.com

Order Information and Rights Permission:

Quantity sales. Special discounts might be available on quantity purchases by corporations, associations, and others. For details, contact the publisher at the address above.

For Book Rights Adaptation and other Rights Permission. Call us at toll-free 1-888-945-8513 or send us an email at admin@stellarliterary.com.

Dedication

I dedicate this testimony to the One who saved me, healed me and called me His own. My Savior, my All is All, Jesus. Without Your grace to guide me, Lord, I would have failed. Those tortuous days, nights and years would have chained me to hell. But Your word told me to get up and put my faith and trust in You.

Your word gave me hope. It gave me a future. When I was weak and ill, Your love comforted me. With faith I believed whatever I say shall be. With faith I rose from that bed of sickness.

Your voice is my light in the darkness and your Word is all I need to break every chain.

Foreword

Whether you're broken and torn or breaking the storm, with faith, this story can heal you. I've lived three decades to write it and I promise it will bless you.

So, to get your attention and check your judgment, I just took a lot of medical marijuana. Judging yet? I didn't think so. But honestly, I really don't know how to function without it…yet. That's how I'm writing this book, not why. I might mention it, but it's not what this story is about. This testimony is about struggles and revivals, victories and chains…and how I'm able to recover from it all. I'm telling my testimony to minister to you, but also to minister to myself. To grow your faith as well as mine. To heal you as well as heal myself…and to encourage you that you are not alone. I'm going to take you through a journey of how my life ended through a traumatic car wreck…and how a new life was created through faith.

Hold on, this is going to be a miraculous ride.

Acknowledgement

Beyond the tragedies I've endured, I am continually blessed by the Saints God has placed in my life:

To my mother, Yvonne Belcastro, and father, Dan Belcastro, thank you. God chose you to be my parents. He chose you because He knew you would sacrifice your lives to better mine. You are the best mom and dad any daughter could ever ask for. I know you love me because you constantly fight for me. As a great example in my life, you are the reason I was able to finish this book and every reason why I am who I am today.

To my husband, Brandon, thank you. You've never given up on me. God chose you to be the man who would stand by my side and fight my every battle. God chose you because He knew you would take care of me. Even out of exhausted frustration you never left me or stopped loving me. You are the one who picked me up off the floor every time I fell. You are the one who sacrificed 12 years of your life to save mine. I could never repay you for the life you gave up for me and our children. But I know God has a plan….to give us hope and a future.

To my brother, Dan J. Belcastro, thank you. Even before the accident, I always looked up to you. You've protected me and encouraged me to never stop trying. I admire your intelligence, patience and kindness. I wouldn't have made it through the most difficult years of my life without you teaching me. You are the best brother I could ever ask for and I know you were chosen by God to give me hope and never give up.

To my Grandma, Betty Watson, thank you. You've always been a role model for me as a hard-working woman. Fancy, intelligent and overpowering with knowledge. I can see through you, how my mom is so strong and intelligent. I thank you grandma for playing a crucial role in mine and my boy's lives. It seems when I was in the most desperate years of my boy's lives, you were there to rescue me. Always at my door to protect me and my babies. I love you and so admire you.

To my dear Grammy, Fannie Belcastro, thank you. Oh, my dear Grammy, what a blessing it would have been to have you by my side at my wedding or my first day of work. What a blessing it would have been to have you by my side when my triplet boys were born…when they said their first words…took their first steps. Oh, my dear Grammy, how I miss every day without you. I think to myself, if only you had been here, but God comforts my heart to remind me that you always were. I love you. I adore you and look forward to the day I get to hug you in heaven.

To my Aunt, Betty Brown, thank you. Thank you for loving me like a daughter. For being strong when I was weak. You were there to comfort me through sickness though you were suffering from illness as well. You put my life before yours and traveled all the way to Denver, Co to stay with me when I was at the deadliest time in my pregnancy. You came all the way to PSL Hospital to care for me so my mom could rest. You put my life before yours. You're a special kind of Saint and I will forever hold that memory in my heart.

To my Aunt, Dianna Sheldon, thank you. You never left my side after the accident, and the sickness. If you hadn't been there to help, take care of my boys, I would have lost them. You've always encouraged me to be strong. You were always here whenever I needed you. I've always admired you for who you are, inside and out. Out of all the people in the world I'd want my life to resemble, it would yours. As a great role model in my life, I thank you for teaching me how to stand and keep standing.

To my mother-in-law, Phyllis Ray, thank you. I have always been able to count on you to care for me and Gavin when I was unable to. You have come to my rescue more times than I can count. I was desperate…but no matter how sad or weak you felt or how much pain you were in, you never turned your back on me. You never left my side. Because of you, I never lost my Gavin.

To my dear Aunt, Yolonda Dorsey, AKA YoYo, thank you. You were there when my Grammy Fannie died. My best friend and yours. Though you were never a replacement, you replaced the pain with joyful memories. I adore you Auntie Yo. I don't know how I would have made it through those miserable days without hearing your voice. Even when I was too weak to pick up the phone, the messages you left filled my heart with hope and that is where you will always be. I wish you were here to witness this, but in heaven, I know you and Grammy already are.

To my Pastors, John and Carla Cappetto, Faith Heights Church, thank you. It is your faith in the word and life-saving messages that have led me to this day. Pastor John, like Abraham, you are a great man of faith. When you preach, I can feel the power of the Holy Spirit fill the room. I feel His love in the scriptures you preach and His presence in the words you speak. You convinced me from the beginning, with the first scriptures you claimed that saved my life. As if God had already planned for that day to be the most memorable day of my life.

Thank you, Pastor Carla. From the first day I walked into the sanctuary, you were there to carry me and catch me when I fell. Like a mother, your concern for me lifted my heart and taught me how to trust God. You were the greatest example of how I want to live my life. You told me to look in the mirror every day and point to myself saying "You are healed by His stripes". You encouraged me to never give up on faith. The presence of God is felt in every word you say and every hug you give.

To Pastors, Mark and Trina Hankins, thank you. Thank you for filling me with the Word and the Holy Spirit. I will never forget the first time I met you. You both spent at least 10 minutes pulling out my pain and filling me with laughter. I was mesmerized by the power that flowed through your fingers and comforted me throughout the night. Hours of laughter cleansed my heart, as fear of darkness escaped me. I was a baby Christian lost in the world until you planted the seeds to straighten my paths. I am forever grateful.

To my best friend, Julie (Seeley) Means, thank you. From the first day I met you at a very young age, I knew we would always be friends. You have always been a great example of how to live like a Christian. How to pray and trust in the power of God. As God knew our futures, he planted every step that led to this day. Like the day your mom taught me the salvation prayer a week before my car wreck. I am blessed to write that you are not only my best friend, but the amazing photographer of every photo in this book. God chose you to be the friend who would never leave my side.

To my friend, Lea Ann Willer, thank you. When I look back at the path God designed to pave this day, I realize it all fell in place the day I meet you. As decades changed, along with my health, you never did. You were there through it all. From the beginning when you purposely scheduled mine and Brandon's appointments at the same time to the day you braided my hair for our wedding. You've sat with me through many trials and tribulations…and here I am, 29 years later, still sitting in your chair.

To my friend, Melissa (Neal) Treto, thank you. My very first friend from the first day of kindergarten. I remember so many adventures we shared as we grew together in elementary school. No matter what, no one could separate us. I remember when I thought living a mile from you was too far away. Lol. Our sleepovers and obsession with Madonna. Matching clothes and matching…hairdos! LOL! I'm so thankful that after all these years, I'm not only your friend, but I'm also your neighbor!

To my friend, Kristina Lague, thank you. I look back at how many times our paths crossed before the day we became friends. From Brandon's concerts to the first day I stepped foot back into a faith-filled church, all I knew of you was your name. As I've watched God bring people in and out of my life, our bond has never broken. Before I even had an accurate diagnosis, you were there to help me fight sickness. Thank you, Kristy. When your son, Jacob came over to play with the boys, when they were all only three years old, our boys formed that same everlasting bond. I admire you and I am mesmerized by your voice. I prayed that one day we would sing together and praise God, He gave me what my heart so desired.

To my friend, Lori Nickel, thank you. I knew from the first day I met you at church, you were chosen by God to walk with me through the deadliest storms. After years and years of trying to figure out how to speak in a tongue, it only took a second in your presence to be filled. As an exhorter, your powerful prayers gave me strength to finish this testimony. You are the only person I know who has suffered in life as much as I have. We were chosen to fight together and win together, my sister in Christ.

To my friend, Brandy Prince, thank you. Thank you for the wisdom and power of God you've engraved in me. I don't think there's a word in the dictionary to describe the admiration I feel towards you. Throughout every Bible class we've shared, I've been inspired by the amount of knowledge God has bestowed in you. The Word of God flows through your mouth like rivers of living water. By equal discernment, a bond will always remain between us, and in the Name of Jesus, nothing can break it.

To my friend, Kelley Hilton, thank you. From the first day we spoke at Faith Heights Church, I knew God had planted a seed to grow a lasting friendship. Thank you for always opening your heart to hear my cries and comfort me through the storms. I look forward to every chance I get to fellowship with you. Every time we come together in prayer; another mountain is moved. Thank you for always filling me with laughter and love.

To my friend Merri Kris, thank you. Thank you for inspiring me to grow in faith and knowledge. Your faith gave me strong hope and hunger for the word. When I finally stepped into God's plan, you were there to guide me. Like a road map God designed to straighten my paths. He chose you to inspire me to join Rhema Bible College and look at where it's taken me! Thank you for teaching me how to have confidence in God's promises to receive whatever I ask for.

To my friend, Moneda Duckworth, thank you. One of the most memorable blessings in my life, after rejoining the workforce, was the day I met you. Full of knowledge, not only in a medical laboratory but also in the things of God. You were the most significant role model in this new walk. My guidance in this new world. I see now that God chose you to lead me to this day. What you taught me 5 years ago has stayed in my heart ever since. Thank you, my friend. You are the one who opened this doorway to my future. With love, you gently pulled me in. My life would never have been the same without you.

To my dearest friend, Cindy Rumpf, thank you. I am blessed to know that after everything we've both been through, we will forever remain friends. Even in the storms, you are joyful. Your sense of humor is admirable. All the days I struggled without an explanation; you were there to bring me laughter on the darkest days. I enjoy every minute I get to spend with you. Though we live far apart, you are always close to my heart.

To my friends, Jon and Rene James, thank you. Rene, God chose you to be the key that opened the door to my faith and unbreakable trust in God. You taught me that even after all the years I've lost, I haven't lost my purpose in life. And Jon, God chose you to be one of my husband's closest friends. Your mercy and love for others shines bright in everything you generously do. You were chosen together to be a light in our darkest days and joy in our victory.

Table of Contents

Chapter One
The End

When I first began to write my testimony, I hated everything about myself. I hated what I had physically and mentally become. After years of studying the Word of God, the only part of my life that I still hate is the reason this happened to me. I've spent almost 3 decades trying to figure out why and I've gotten nowhere. All I can remember is that horrific night.

Darkness filled the sky on a desolate highway, and I am reminded of that darkness every morning when I wake up weak and ill. Every time I have to swallow the pills and inject the medications that keep me "alive" and "replace" what was taken from me. It never has and I can't imagine how it ever could. I will never be the same. This is the biggest chapter in my life, and I wish I could shred every single page.

I remember the freedom I felt when I drove off in my 16th birthday present. It was the beginning of a bright new future I worked so hard to achieve. I planned to graduate from high school in my junior year and receive a scholarship to Harvard or Yale. I wanted to be a scientist. Possibly a Neurologist. I wanted to take away the pain that was engulfed in anyone with a disability. I was consumed by a strong sympathy for the disabled students in my class. But I had no idea that months later, I would be one of them. My sympathy quickly turned into empathy.

In every daily struggle, I'm trying to love this new me, but I haven't figured out how. I really don't want to accept this. I just want to go back..... July 26, 1993. That date is imprinted in my brain. The lights, the tree and the darkness. The only memory of that night is standing by my car asking my boyfriend to drive me home. I don't remember why but he said no and that I do remember. I got off work…. had dinner with my boyfriend's family…took a nap…drove home…where did it all go wrong? What if I had left a minute later…. a minute earlier? A tough reality to face. I will never know in this lifetime.

It was a warm night. Stars filled the sky. I remember driving, singing and envisioning my future. Life was good and then it happened. Flashing bright lights and nowhere to turn. A head on collision and a broken soul. I was left in a pool of blood with no one around but the man who stole my life. As I lay in a coma, choking on blood from a shattered jaw, he decided to steal more than my life. My CD's, birthday money, the new watch on my wrist…even the new shoes on my feet. Then he left. He just left me there to die.

I was planted in a shallow grave beneath my car after it flipped several times. My seatbelt broke loose from the impact, and I was ejected through the driver's side window, shattering my jaw. I obviously do not remember the sound of my car rolling. I don't remember how it felt to break a window with my jaw…I don't even remember falling out of the window when my seatbelt broke loose. I don't remember sliding into a shallow ditch, when my car fell on top of me. I don't even remember screaming out of shock as the paramedics lifted me onto the care flight. It was past midnight, and my mom was driving toward the accident in search for me. She arrived just in time to hear every scream. She had told me that she ran to the helicopter, but the paramedics wouldn't let her in. I can't imagine the fear my parents must have felt as they drove for 30 minutes from the accident to St. Mary's Hospital.

I was flown to our most advanced hospital in Grand Junction, Co, where I remained in a coma for 2 months. I don't know anything that took place during that time, but I've heard the stories. My mom told me how strong I was even in a coma. I fought the entire time, and I never gave up.

I've lost sight of the day I opened my eyes, as I was severely drugged and weak from the side effects of being left beaten to death by a drunken driver. I could barely see or hear, and I had no words to speak. If I had, they would have been, Where? Who? Why? What? Wondering where I was, who I was and why those people surrounding me were staring at me and what the what is happening? My mind had erased each verb and every noun.

I didn't react because I didn't know how. I couldn't open my mouth to scream, and my mind was blank. I needed answers but I had no idea how to ask. I wreaked my brain trying to comprehend what was happening to me. I was exhausted but I had slept for so long I couldn't sleep anymore. By the end of every confusing day, while my mom was in the other bed in Hilltop Rehab Center, I would stay awake all night and play with the stuffed animals visitors brought me. I was a child again.

My mom would turn on the TV, but I couldn't contemplate one word coming through the speakers. I had no words to say, and no one spoke a language I could understand.

I had many visitors, but out of all the people who came to my room every day, there was only one I remembered. He was the last person I saw. The last person I touched….and the first person to break my heart… my boyfriend. I felt embarrassed as soon as he walked into my hospital room. Out of all the pain, anger and confusion, the strongest emotion I felt was fear. Fear of losing the only part of my life I could understand. The only part I could remember. I panicked the first time he looked at me. I was broken and torn. Desperate for his acceptance and then he was gone. I was lost without a word to say.

With daily rehab and therapy, I relearned how to walk, talk and feed myself again…after removing the wires that held my face together, that is. I relearned all of this with double vision. You realize the head injury is massive when the side effects are multi-vision. Everything I looked at duplicated itself two to six times. I was forced to wear an eye patch over my left eye to block out the blur and strengthen my sight. All I could do was wait through the months of testing and healing.

There was documented hearing loss, but it wasn't severe…yet.

As the months went by, I could finally open my mouth, but I didn't know enough words to form a sentence. Actually, I didn't know ANY words. Due to the partial damage to my frontal cortex, which is responsible for processing nouns, it was extremely difficult for me to converse with others. Ironically, I more easily relearned verbs. For instance, I could say "open" but I had no idea how to say "door". It would take me at least 5 minutes to say a sentence because I couldn't remember the word for the person, place or thing. I didn't know how to say a correct sentence or ask a simple question. I didn't know how to tell anyone how weak, thirsty and confused I felt. At that moment, I didn't know anything but verbs.

For a short while, I used my hands to talk for me. As time went by, the healing in my body and my brain began to progress. I was able to relearn and consume information. I couldn't talk that well, but I could type. Typing was the first lesson I started in rehab. I typed and typed until I could finally read the words. Though I had a hard time writing a sentence, my typing speed was over 400 wpm. With daily rehab, speech therapy and occupational therapy, I relearned enough in one year to return to my senior year and graduate with my class. I couldn't have done any of this without my parents…. who took me almost a year to recall.

I struggle to forget the day I walked back into that high school. I can still feel the lapse as my identity was ripped from me. An honor student one day and in special education the next. I was instantly consumed by fear right when I sat down. The teacher asked us to practice writing our name…. So, I stood up and said, "I don't belong here"! I was so ashamed and so embarrassed to return to a school where I was once esteemed. No one understood what I had physically gone through. I walked and talked and moved much slower than everyone else. I had two massive head injuries, what did they expect? I was mocked and made fun of by the very people who used to call me their friend. The same people who used to call me Dr. Belcastro. They witnessed my achievements and then marked me as Dr. Retard. I was changed that day. I was unacceptable to them, so I was unacceptable to myself. I allowed their opinions to alter my future.

I didn't know who I was or who I was supposed to be for 26 years, but I remember what it felt like to be free from bondage. To be able to jump out of bed in excitement for a new day. To look forward to each year. I remember how my life was supposed to turn out. I remember, and that's why I've spent every single day since, in a deep depression. A depression that only faith could break…

Faith…that is the most significant concept in every individual life. Believing you were meant for more and if you believe with all your heart, you can have whatever you ask for. (See Mark 11:23-24 ESV). That seems like a simple solution to the failures that life can bring us. If only there wasn't an adversary seeking to devour me every single day. (See 1 Peter 5:8 ESV).

Some days, I'm blessed with the energy to speak. Knowledge in the Word opens my mouth to claim, what I say shall be. (See Proverbs 15:2 ESV). These faith-filled days are the only days I live for….to feel His healing power surround me. I reach out my hands to take hold, but it invariably slips through my fingers.

I've tried being the smartest. I've tried being the fastest. I've even tried being the strongest. But trying to be a Christian is the hardest type of person I've ever tried to be. It's a never-ending glory sparked by a fragment of understanding and fulfilled by a pea size of faith. I know my faith is bigger than a pea! So, now's the hard part…. I have to keep the faith, and this is just the beginning.

Chapter Two
Shamed

T rust in the Lord with all your heart, and do not lean on your own understanding. In all your ways acknowledge him, and he will make straight your paths.

Proverbs 3:5-6 (ESV)

Raised in a Catholic cathedral and I had no understanding of that scripture. After years of catechism, I began to fear God and believe that if I sinned, I would be punished. According to Kenneth E. Hagin, the catholic church is divided into two groups, Calvinists and Arminians. Calvinists embrace predestination. For example, they believed that if you were predestined to be saved, you'd be saved but if not, there was nothing you could do about it. Arminians have the idea that God is always out to get you. Like God's constantly waiting for you to mess up so He can punish you. I would surely relate my experience in a Catholic culture to Arminians. For so many years I thought God hated me. I never learned how to receive God's outpouring. How to fill my heart with His mercy and grace. I never learned the love of God until I joined a faith-based church. It was there that I learned the truth, God Actually loves me. (See 1 John 4:16 (ESV). Before I finally understood this concept, I really didn't know God and I had no relationship with Him. All the years in that cultish cliche. I wasn't even taught how to pray when I awoke. I wasn't taught that the blood of Jesus cleanses all our sins. (See 1 John 1:7). It was ignorance that kept me from claiming the Word of God over my life. I never knew how to trust in His power. Out of lack of knowledge and fatigue, I never allowed myself. It was my mom's faith that kept me alive that day. …that day….

It was about a twenty-minute drive home from my boyfriend's house. My dad is a farmer and owns many acres in New Liberty, Colorado. Maybe the distance was too long…. or maybe, I was just inexperienced. I remember that warm summer evening. The desolate road and the darkened sky. A light breeze blew against my skin and in a flash of a second, my life replaced a minute of freedom for three decades of confinement.

Lights engulfed me with nowhere to turn…. That is the last I can recall of July 26, 1993. But I will never forget the life that was taken from me that dark and lonely night.

A broken hip and shattered jaw. I was left to die and bound in shock as I choked on blood. Though I know who did this to me, I still haven't received justice for his actions. The state patrolman on duty looked past the blue paint on my light green car and said I fell asleep. No justice. Left to die. Left to blame even though I was blameless. Left to wonder my entire life. Why did this happen to me?

Proverbs 21:15 (ESV), it says, "When justice is done, it is a joy to the righteous but terror to the evildoers".

So, I'm left to ask, where is my justice?

It was past midnight, and my parents were in panic. My mom drove off to find me, but she was too late and for months, all she could do is watch over me as I lay unconscious of the world and unaware of my life to come. Then I awoke…paralyzed, partially deaf, partially blind and surrounded by people who loved me, but I had no idea who they were. I didn't even know who I was. I didn't know who anyone was. I guess that wasn't important at the time since I had no idea how to talk and my teeth were wired shut. I was unaware of that as well. Apparently so were the nurses because they constantly tried to pry my mouth open to swallow pills. I'm curious as to how much of my history was shared during rounds because I hadn't even relearned how to swallow yet. My mom was there to rescue me every time though. She never left my side. If she had, I doubt I would have lived to share my story.

Friends would drop by to show me pictures. My best friend, Julie, even made an album for me. I didn't know who she was either and refused to believe that the person standing next to her in the pictures was me. It took me almost a year to remember.

I will never forget the day I finally relearned the alphabet. My mom sang me the ABC song and I sang along. I ran to wake up my dad from a nap to sing to him. I'll never forget his smile.

I had to relearn everything. Honestly, everything. My parents' house had signs on every "thing". Fork…. spoon…. door…. etc. Their house looked like a Neuro/Trauma unit. Physical Therapist, Occupational Therapist…. Nurses and doctors and it never ended.

I lost everything without a fair trial. I never received the honors I deserved for the years of study I endured. I never received anything in return for the future he stole from me. I couldn't believe what my life had become. I worked so hard for that day to hear "Victoria Belcastro, Harvard University"! But that day never came. My family still held a party for my graduation. They were proud of me but all I could feel was shame. Everyone is laughing and smiling as if I "accomplished" something. It's hard to smile when you feel broken and hopeless. I was meant for so much more. But, throughout every disappointment I faced, I still had hope.

I had hope even in the beginning when I was forced to visit doctors and psychologists daily. Why would they send me to a psychologist when I hadn't even relearned how to talk yet? As a newly brain injured teen, I was very gullible. After an entire year, the ONLY thing I can recall the psychologist saying to me, is that my trip to heaven was just a dream. Maybe my life would have been different if I hadn't believed her.

The doctors would tell me that if I tried hard enough, I could be exactly who I was before the accident. I actually believed them! Well after 27 years of sickness…no I'm not the same. Out of all the lines the doctors fed me, they still didn't know how to diagnose me correctly. The only obvious sign was my infatuation with water. So, they scheduled an observation with the best Endocrinologist, Dr. Joseph Maruca. After numerous blood tests and MRI's, I was, eventually, diagnosed with panhypopituitarism, diabetes insipidus (water diabetes) and hypothalamic seizures.

The pituitary gland is the master gland. The hormones created and released by the glands in your body's endocrine system control nearly all the processes in your body. So, as you can imagine, I was instantly prescribed a ton of medications to replace everything my body didn't make on its own. For most of my life I've lived on prescription drugs. These medications were meant to help me but after taking them for so many years, they've become more of a harm. The symptoms of these deficiencies cause weakness, thirst and fear. The pituitary produces hormones that stimulate the adrenal glands. I feel weak from adrenal failure, dehydrated from insipidus and terrified of having another seizure.

Adrenal Failure is the most obvious explanation for the constant fatigue. The adrenal glands are responsible for producing aldosterone, cortisol, and adrenaline. Cortisol is a stress hormone, essential for life. Adrenaline is known as the "fight-or-flight hormone". It is released in response to stress, pain, excitement and danger. Adrenaline helps your body react more quickly, makes the heartbeat faster and increases blood flow to your brain and muscles. It also produces sugar to use for fuel....but I've lost my fuel. I've lost my fuel and I'm dragging in somnolence and desiccation.

The type of seizures I'm diagnosed with are called hypothalamic seizures. They are caused by damage to my hypothalamus. When the electric waves circling around my brain shock the fear section, the terrifying experience that follows is indescribable. It's an out of body experience and all I can feel is panic as evil attacks me. During these seizures, I'm usually too weak and afraid to speak, but sometimes I'm strong. I can feel the seizures coming on and I instantly say the name of Jesus. When I say his name, the seizures only last a second or two but when I'm too weak to open my mouth, satan's fiery darts drown me in darkness for hours.

Many people have opinions as to what I can accomplish during a seizure. I had my first seizure when I was in a coma at 16. I opened my eyes and my mom thought I was waking up from the coma, but my eyes rolled back in my head, and I had a grand mal seizure. A few years after I awoke, I was diagnosed with generalized onset seizures, referred to as, Absence Seizures, or Petit Mal Seizures. These forms of seizures are non-epileptic. Petit Mal Seizures typically only last a few seconds. They can cause you to blink repeatedly or stare into space. That's why my doctor thought I was just daydreaming. It took years for my doctors to recognize it as seizures. They missed the signs and wrongly diagnosed it as panic attacks. In my case, I have learned to stay focused during a seizure. I used to stare off trying to stop it with my own mind. I didn't have to stare. That was a choice. I could talk and work and have a seizure at the same time because I learned how to be a functioning… "seizure-holic". Even on seizure meds a Petit Mal Seizure would break though one to ten times a day depending on my strength to endure another episode.

I remember the first seizure I had two years after I awoke from the coma. I was working for Dr. Maruca. He hired me to teach me how to function in society. I remember, I was in the front office sitting at a computer when fear hit me, and I went blank and stared off for minutes while the doctor continued to call out my name. After witnessing my first episode, Dr. Maruca referred me to a psychologist, assuming I was having panic attacks. My first appointment with this doctor was quite awkward. I thought I would have someone to talk to about how broken I was but I found out that this appointment was just an evaluation to prescribe a suitable anti-depressant. One day, after a week of following the psychologist's orders to ingest Zoloft, my right arm began to shake uncontrollably. My mom drove me to the hospital, and I was instantly hooked up on an EEG machine to check for seizures. There it was. All along. I wasn't having panic attacks. I was having seizures. I look back at the steps it took to come to an accurate conclusion. It only took a psychologist prescribing me Zoloft to piece it together.

Out of all the deficiencies I've been diagnosed with, and all the medications I've been prescribed, there is only one pharmaceutical drug that keeps me alive, Cortisone, previously described as "essential for life". Cortisone Acetate is a synthetic corticosteroid with many side effects, and I've been taking it for almost thirty years. The symptoms of this drug are debilitating, for me. Yet, this drug is all I have to survive....

...It wasn't until 2001 that the signs and symptoms of my diagnosis's began to control my life. I gradually became severely fatigued in fear. By 2005 I was so weak I could no longer take care of myself. My endocrinologist tried every pill in the pharmacy to get me out of bed but nothing worked. So, there I lay, bedridden for over a decade.

Chapter Three
A New Life

An imaginary Tick- Tock -Tick- Tock....was all I heard as the days, nights and years of my life slowly faded away. It was 2003 and my new norm was fatigue. My entire life was engulfed in it and by 2005 silence and darkness were my only friends. As dawn turned to morning and morning into night, they began to speak to me. The voices were echoing inside the walls but only I could hear them. Assured to appear at the same exact time every single night. I awaited each hour in fear, unaware of what to come...

I had seen the best endocrinologist in the United States and not one of them had the cure. Every answer remained the same, "there's nothing more we can do", "but let's change all your medications around and make your life even more miserable"! Or "let's fill your blood and brain with every stimulant we can prescribe". It seems every stimulant they gave me, was prescribed to treat ADD, attention-deficit disorder. So, oddly, after years of taking stimulants, I developed ADD. I don't know why I feel like laughing at that. Now that I think about it, I'm surprisingly thankful for the ADD, regarding my circumstances. See the ADD caused OCD, obsessive compulsive disorder, and the OCD got me out of bed. My biggest obsession was washing my hands. I may have also appropriated this obsession from working in a medical laboratory, but it got much worse...but it got me out of bed. So, I developed a system and became obsessed with fifteen-minute intervals. I had to get out of bed at a certain time and if I didn't get out of bed, for example, at exactly 6, I had to wait until 6:15 and if I couldn't get out of bed at 6:15, I had to wait until 6:30, etc. This habit made me late almost every day, but it was my first experiment. Ugh, the fatigue.

The drug responsible for the foolish traits I acquired was phentermine. This medication releases high levels of dopamine, norepinephrine and serotonin to increase energy, you know, like speed! That is exactly how it felt. These pills gave me superhuman powers, like I broke through the windows of a lab experiment. I didn't realize the effects it was causing by overstimulating my adrenal glands. The result was aggressive anger. I remember the first time I experienced this intense anger. I don't know what my husband, Brandon, did to make me so mad, this was years ago, but I turned into the hulk and threw a 150-pound coffee table across the room at him. I'll never forget the look on his face. He wasn't even mad. He was more amazed.

One night, after working a 10-hour shift at the lab, I was so high on phentermine, I lifted our couch with one hand to vacuum under it. That look on Brandon's face again. Lol!

This amphetamine, phentermine, was prescribed to be taken for 10 days. My doctor prescribed it for over 10 years. I understand the reason why, now. It was because there were no other treatments available. Dr. Maruca had already tried them all. I remember, immediately after my first dose, I felt like I was on high school track again. I felt like I was constantly running. It was a synthetic form of adrenal like I had never felt before. I could work twice as hard as everyone else in a hospital laboratory. I could get out of bed and have a life! I could multi-task like no one else. I felt powerful and though I was full of toxins, I felt healthy. It was amazing. I was so strong. Every day after work I would go to the gym and take two aerobic classes in a row…. and then, suddenly, after a couple years, it was gone. I lost it all, again. I crashed and I crashed hard. Out of nowhere, my body began to reject this energy "supplement". My strength eventually became my greatest weakness. As a result of adrenal failure, the only way for me to gain stamina was to become angry and though the phentermine aided in increasing my anger, my doctor continued to recommend it.

He was my care giver, and I thought the world of him. I trusted in his education and every word he said. I argued with my family as they continually flushed my phentermine down the toilet like I was some drug addict…was I? No matter what my family did to stop me from taking it, my doctor always gave me more at the highest dose, 37.5 mg. I know he didn't do this to hurt me. He honestly believed he was helping me, while he watched the side effects of phentermine and adrenal failure destroy me.

I had to plan a new life around this deficiency. I never knew when I was going to wake up from the coma, I fell into every single time I fell asleep. I hated the fatigue and exhaustion weighing on me. I felt like I was suffocating under piles of blankets that chained me to my bed. I would tell everyone "I have mental energy but no physical energy". I would lay in bed some days and just imagine myself walking. I would imagine myself thriving. I would imagine myself well…but somehow, my physical weakness was always stronger than my imagination.

My circadian rhythm was backward and the only time I had any energy was at night. But again, I only had mental energy and remained bedridden. Circadian rhythm is controlled by the hypothalamus. It is a natural, internal process that regulates the sleep-wake cycle and repeats every 24 hours. The hypothalamus also regulates the pituitary gland by sending messages. It is situated immediately above the "master" gland.

By 2001 I was up all night, and I slept all day. You would think I was something of a party animal. But quite the opposite. I only left my bed if it was prescheduled, and I stayed up for at least an entire day to make sure I didn't miss appointments. See, once I fell asleep, I couldn't wake up from the fatigue that kept me strapped to that bed. I wasn't irresponsible, I was just extremely weak. But no one seemed to understand, as sickness and side effects erased six more years of my life.

It was 2007 and I was still bedridden. The years escaped me in a glance. When you wake up alone every day, every other day, or every other week, you feel desperate and isolated. My husband was there after work and on the weekends but other than that, I found no reason to fight just to wake up. I began to grow weaker and weaker and more and more, lonely. One day, my dad said, "If you're so lonely, why don't you just have a baby".

20

He said it like "just have a baby". The idea sank into my heart, and I soon decided I didn't want to be alone anymore. I thought "If I had a baby, it would cause me to get out of bed every day and we could thrive together". It was everything I ever wanted. I spoke to my endocrinologist, and he sent me to a reproductive endocrinologist in Denver, Co.

I stayed in Denver, Co for three months to receive injections to stimulate my ovaries. My stomach was swollen within a couple days from the injections, and I looked like I was already pregnant. I really didn't know what to say when people asked me how far a-long I was. It took several months of infertility treatment to prepare for the day of insemination. I remember when the nurses were skeptical as to whether just one insemination would be enough. So, they doubled the dose. It took a while to get news as to whether the insemination was successful. But after the wait, a nurse finally called me and my mom at the hotel. She said the best words I had ever heard. "Congratulations, you're pregnant." I was so excited to call my husband, Brandon, and tell him this miraculous news.

I truly believed my life was finally turning around for the better. But it wasn't until my first ultrasound, one week later, that I was proven wrong. The screen showed multiple images. Brandon and I were unable to piece it together. The doctor finally turned up the ultrasound so we could hear. The OB/GYN said, "three heart beats"! I was overwhelmed with joy, until she said "You need to reduce" …. as if they were disposable. Even though I was not with God at the time, I never agreed with abortion. So, I said, "No way I didn't go through all of this to kill my babies". The OB/GYN continued to argue that if I followed through with this pregnancy, it would eventually kill me. I looked over at Brandon and I could sense fear in his eyes as the doctor rambled on. But there was nothing she could say to change my mind. I was unaware of faith but following God's plan, even though everything the doctor said would happen came to be. I was immediately ordered to remain in bedrest.

There I lay, confined to a bed and bronzed with shackles once again.

21

I remained bedridden throughout my entire pregnancy. I remained locked in my bed for six months, 24 hours a day, during my pregnancy. The doctors were impressed with the fact that I followed their orders. They were so inspired, yet they had no idea that I had already been chained to that bed for years. As months went by, I began to develop bed sores, muscle weakness, increased deafness and blindness… and the pain grew worse by the day. I was in constant pain throughout it all. My ovaries would fill up with fluid and cause excessive pain. My mom would drive 4-5 hours to my reproductive endocrinologist office in Denver, Co, to drain my ovaries. I was in so much pain throughout the entire procedure, but only the doctor performing it understood why. This went on so many times, that after 18 weeks of pregnancy, I was finally placed in a high-risk unit in Colorado Springs, Co., Memorial Hospital.

When I was diagnosed with adrenal failure, I was prescribed Cortisone Acetate to replace the corticosteroids that my adrenal glands no longer made on their own. Corticosteroids also regulate your response to stress, inflammation, metabolism, immunity and pain control. It was the only medication that kept me alive after the car wreck. As an adrenal replacement, Cortisone is synthetic and harmful to the embryo during any stage of development. The first Endocrinologist I saw in Colorado Springs, Co. wanted to cut my dose in half. Thankfully the High-Risk Pregnancy Specialist at Memorial Hospital knew that at that low of a dose of Cortisone, I would become too weak to carry the babies. Without the Cortisone I would have no adrenal function. So, my recommended daily dose was never changed, but my babies absorbed it all to survive. The effects kicked in with depression and unbearable pain. The nurses constantly drugged me with sleeping pills. I was strongly sedated to block the non-stop, intense pain I endured. Even the ultrasounds were painful. Since it was a high-risk pregnancy, I had to have six every day. The nurses watched me suffer in agony but refused to understand why. I was too ill to thrive, and my last ultrasound showed that my babies were not doing well.

I loved my Neo-natal specialist from Memorial Hospital in Colorado Springs, Co. He would drive to Grand Junction every six weeks to consult with high-risk moms. After seeing me for the first time and viewing my ultrasound, he informed me that I needed to be in a high-risk Neo-natal unit. He made the arrangements for me to continue my pregnancy on bed rest at his hospital. He took extraordinary care of me during my 3.5 week stay. My mom and my specialist watched me suffer that entire time because he couldn't find an endocrinologist that would make hospital visits. My mom prayed and God clearly told her that I needed to be in a more advanced high-risk hospital. The specialist agreed and moved me to a hospital in Denver, Co. My new endocrinologist instantly knew how to care for me. He came to my room every day. Each and every doctor that cared for me, was chosen by God.

My mom's faith placed me and my babies in the best high-risk Neo-natal unit at Presbyterian St Luke's Hospital in Denver, Co. I so wish I had allowed God in my life before my pregnancy but thankfully my mom did. God was there the whole time protecting me and my boys. I was blessed with the best reproductive endocrinologist, Neo-natal specialist and endocrinologist throughout my entire pregnancy.

I didn't know how to have faith in my own prayers, but I had faith in my mom's. As a servant of God, she always has her ears inclined to hear from Him. She surrendered to His call, and He marked my every step…. but I constantly tripped.

After being placed at PSL Hospital, I was instantly surrounded by women who were pregnant with multiples. The therapists would take us to a maternity pool to relax every day. I stayed in that hospital for five months and only made it to the pool twice. I was so weak and so sick. I didn't have enough air in my lungs to speak. I was sure I was dying but I was determined to protect my babies. I wouldn't allow them to die with me.

At 24 weeks I was forced to increase my oxygen and learn how to sleep sitting up. The acid in my throat and stomach constantly burned. Even a small sip of water would put me in tears. I couldn't eat, I couldn't drink and I couldn't sleep. And by the 26th week, I could barely see or hear. I was quickly slipping away. The nurses and psychologist came in my room constantly and I couldn't take it anymore. They were trying to prove to me that I was just depressed. Not one nurse who came in my room could even consider the amount of suffering I was going through. They didn't understand, so I was left to suffer for another two weeks.

I remember getting into my freshly changed hospital bed. It was late, October 19, 2007, and I had finally reached 28 weeks. I had just been given a bath and was holding on strong to keep my babies alive. Immediately after laying down, I told my mom "I think I just peed the bed and it smells like saline solutions". She said, "oh no, your water broke". I was caught up in the excitement but worried I wouldn't live to hold my babies. My mom ran out of my room and called for a nurse. A ton of nurses rushed into my room. I called Brandon in Grand Junction, Co. He rushed through the snowy mountains to be there for his children's birth.

The nurses ran in and immediately started the ultrasound. They were able to see that baby B had broken his sac. After testing, the doctors discovered that our amniotic fluid was infected, and we were all dying. I was rushed to the delivery room. There were 2 neo-natal doctors and 2 nurses per baby. I received 3 shots in the spine from the anesthesiologist and became paralyzed from the neck down. I instantly freaked out as my heart rate escalated. I was on so many sleeping pills I could barely stay awake. I began to panic. I could see the light. I knew I was going to die. The anesthesiologist and my mom stood right beside me, constantly telling me to open my eyes and keep breathing. I was on baby aspirin for the babies, and I was bleeding excessively from the cesarean. I was bleeding faster than the transfusion could filter into my bloodstream. I was becoming weaker and weaker. The nurses showed me baby B and baby C but baby A was stillborn and rushed to NICU. My soul was empty, and I gave up the ghost.

I thought it was over. I thought I was done suffering. I thought if I left a piece of myself with my family, they would let me die. I fought to keep them alive, and I fought to keep myself alive. All for them. I know my soul left my body at 0233 that early morning. My family refuses to believe it. Only I remember the fire. I opened my eyes and once again, I felt betrayed and more alone than I had ever felt in my life. My babies weren't with me anymore. They were unreachable inside isolettes. Locked up in NICU.

My husband, Brandon, arrived 30 minutes too late to witness his multiples birth. He drove to Denver in three hours, in the snow, and was right by my side when I awoke from darkness. As soon as I was able to, he wheeled me to NICU to meet my babies. I sat and stared at my boys in their incubators for hours. It was love at first sight. They were so small and even though I couldn't feel their heartbeat against mine anymore, I could still feel the bond between us. I wasn't allowed to hold my babies for three months. I was only allowed to lay one hand on their head or stick out one finger for them to hold on to. The pain in my heart was overwhelmed as the nurses wheeled me back to my room. I cried as they pushed me down the hall. At every angle I could see a happy mom holding their newborn baby while mine were chained in a cage. My babies were sick like me, and I had no faith in saving them.

I was surrounded by strength in the presence of my mom and comforted by the faith in my best friend's prayers. My mom would guide me throughout each day. She would feed me. Help me out of bed. Bathe me…medicate me…she did everything for me. She always has. I trusted in her to make me physically and mentally strong every day. But on the days when I had no strength at all, I put all my faith in my best friend, Julie, to comfort me. Her knowledge of the Bible and her confidence in the power of Christ was all I had to stand on. And her prayers gave me hope in a savior.

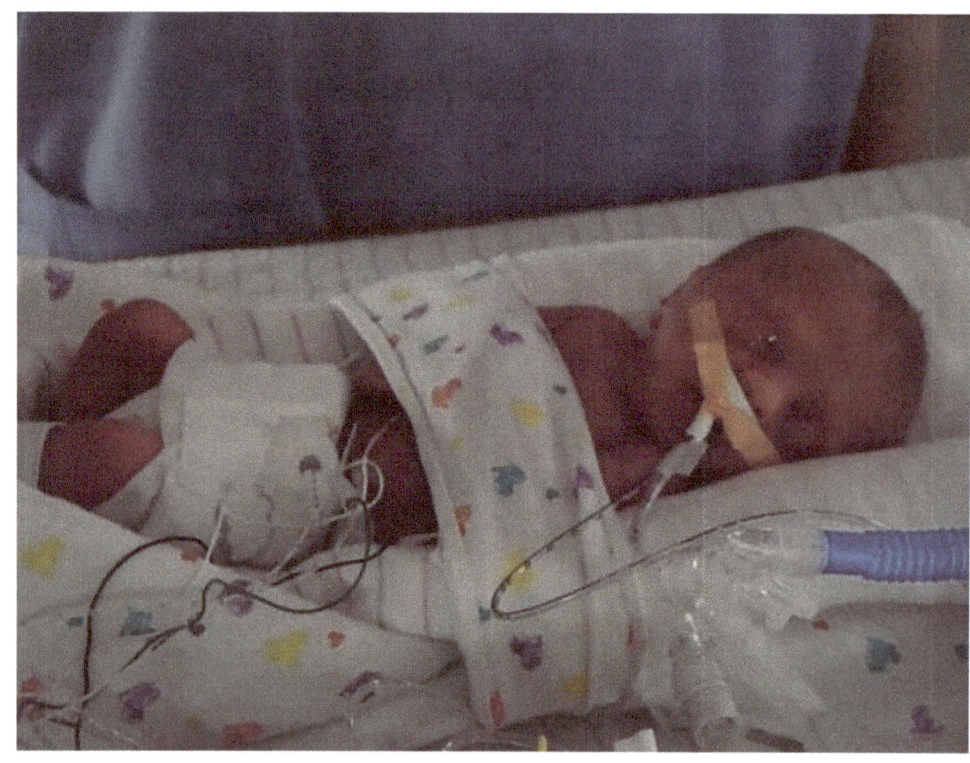

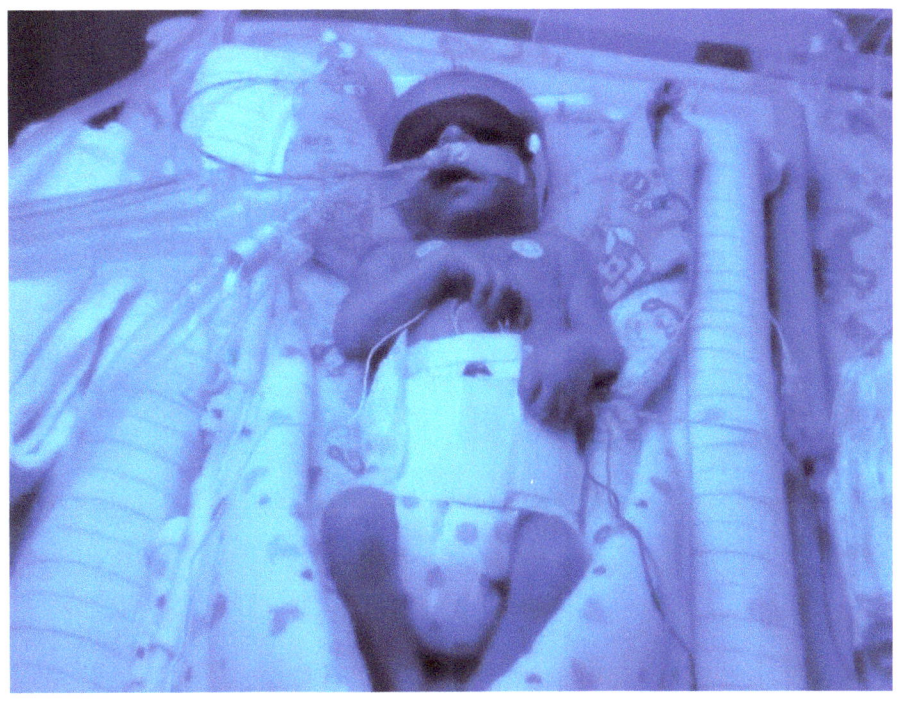

Jayden Angelo, Baby A, was born weighing 2 lbs. 9 oz. Jayden was stillborn and tagged with a multitude of complications. The infected amniotic fluid slowed the development of his lungs, and he was diagnosed with Chronic Lung Disease. As I sat through his daily tests and transfusions, I would imagine him well. When he was back in his isolate in NICU, I would sit and stare at him and wait for him to finally open his eyes. We were told every day that Jayden was going to die. My heart was so attached but whenever I felt the fear of losing him, the power surrounding and protecting him grew even stronger. I awaited in hope and after three months I finally got to hold my little miracle.

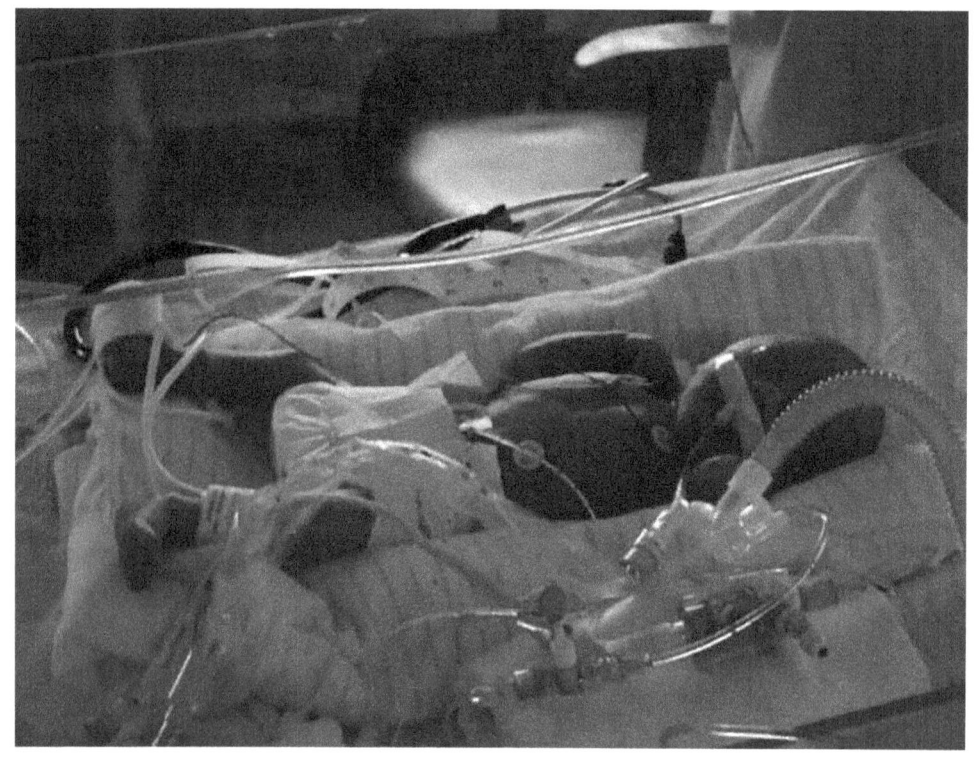

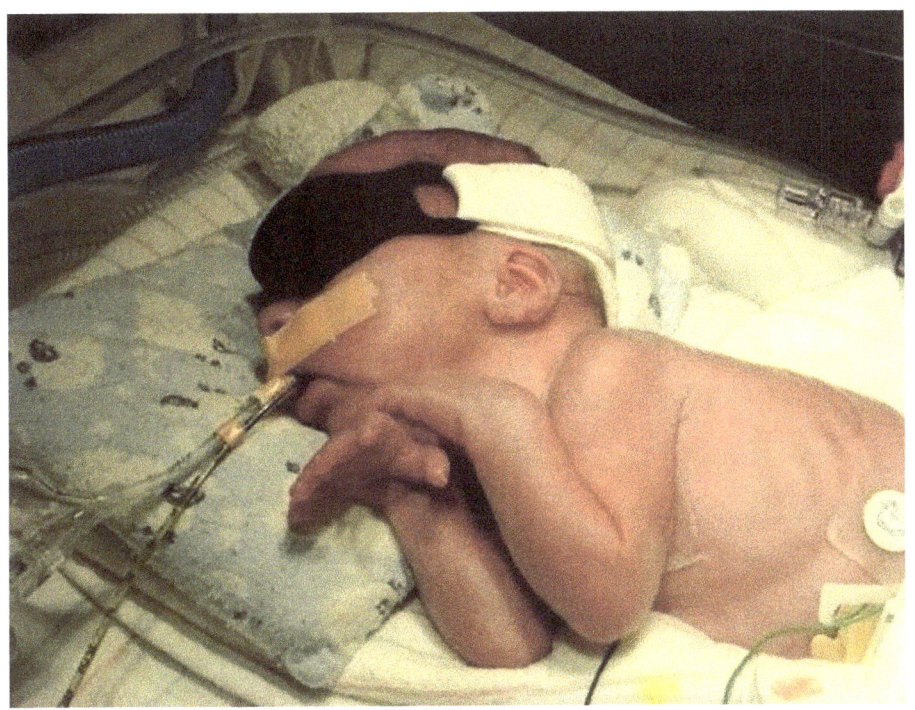

My second baby, Baby B, Dominic Nico, was only 2 lbs. 13 oz. and was also born with a list of problems. His most prominent issue was a huge hole in his heart, but it miraculously closed on its own. He saved our lives, and he will forever be our hero. After two months, I finally got to hold my handsome boy, "Dominico". He was the first baby I was allowed to hold. My heart was overjoyed as I realized how much he resembled me. I will never forget that joyful day when I finally felt the comfort I had so strongly desired, as I held his precious little body in my arms.

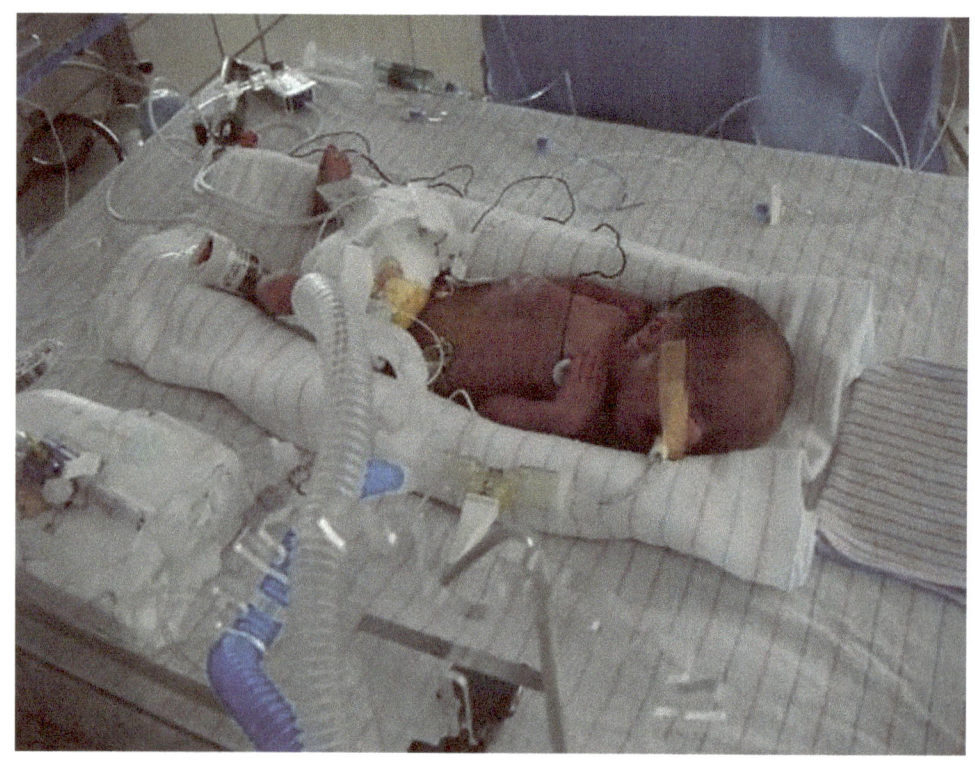

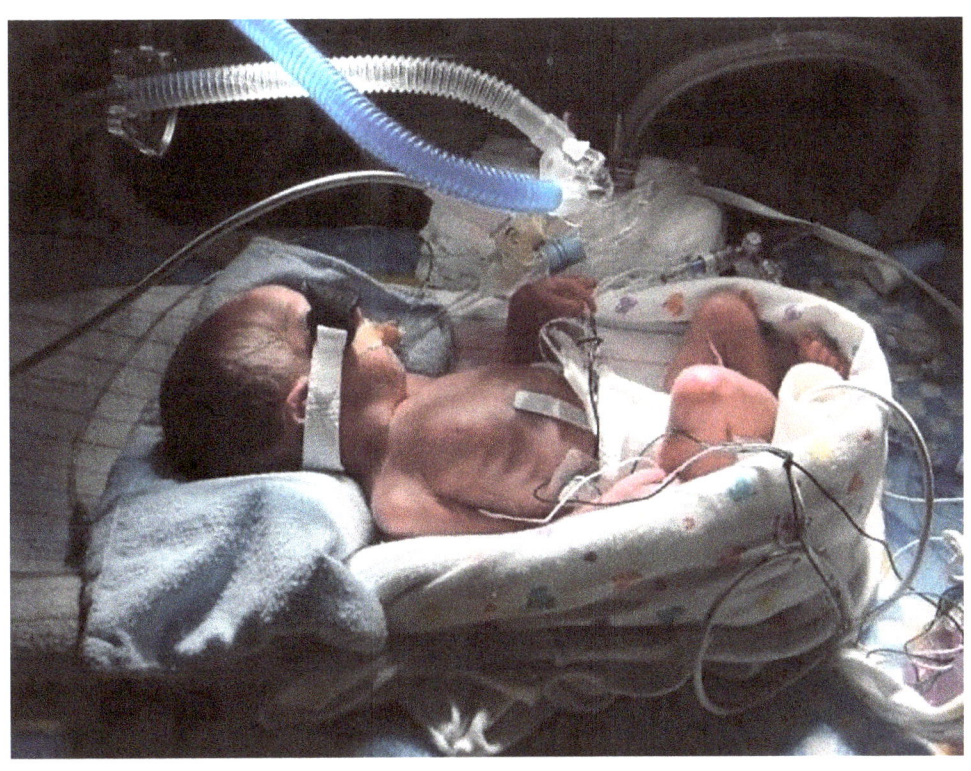

Even though Baby C, Gavin Gianni, was only 1 lb. 14 oz., he was the healthiest baby of the three. We didn't have to worry about him as much. I loved to hold his tiny little hand and run my fingers through his thick black hair. Though he was so small, I knew in my heart that he was going to live. He was the second baby I was allowed to hold. I looked into his beautiful blue eyes as if I was looking right into Brandon's. I instantly knew that, just like his Daddy, he would always protect me.

After four months, we finally brought our babies home.

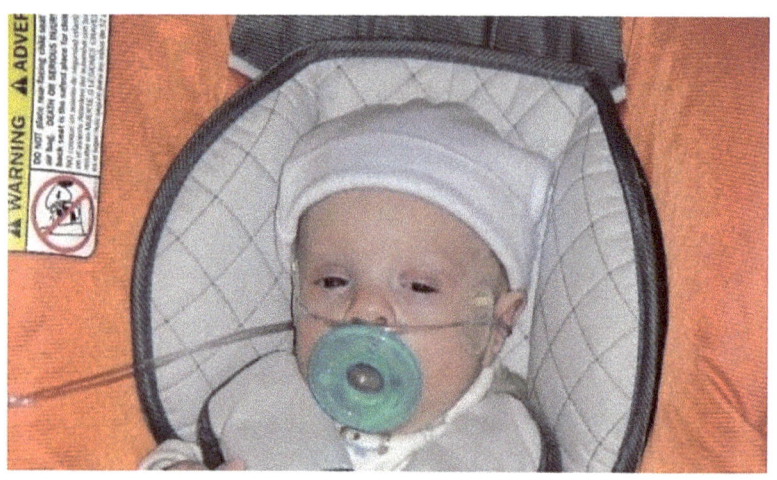

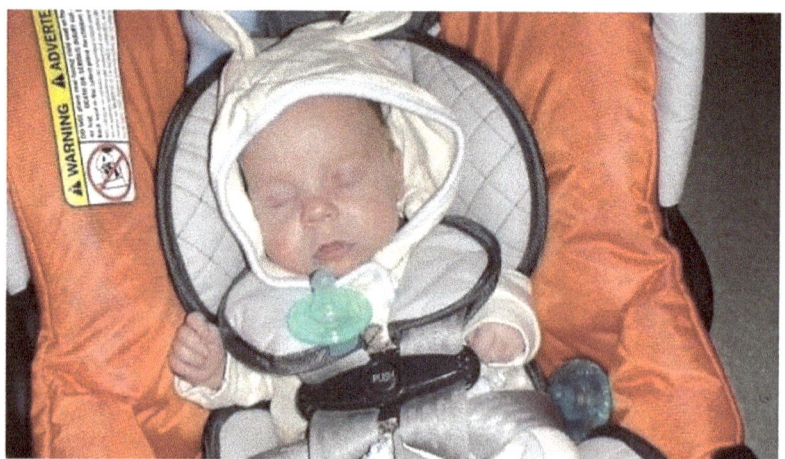

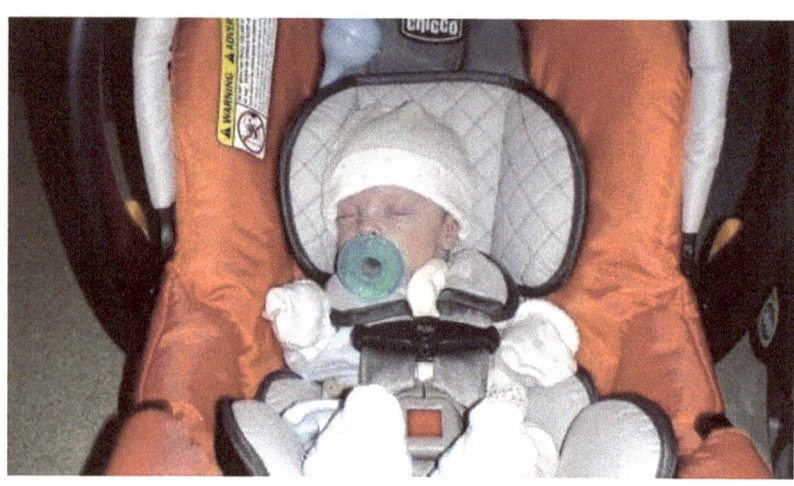

Chapter Four
Utter Darkness

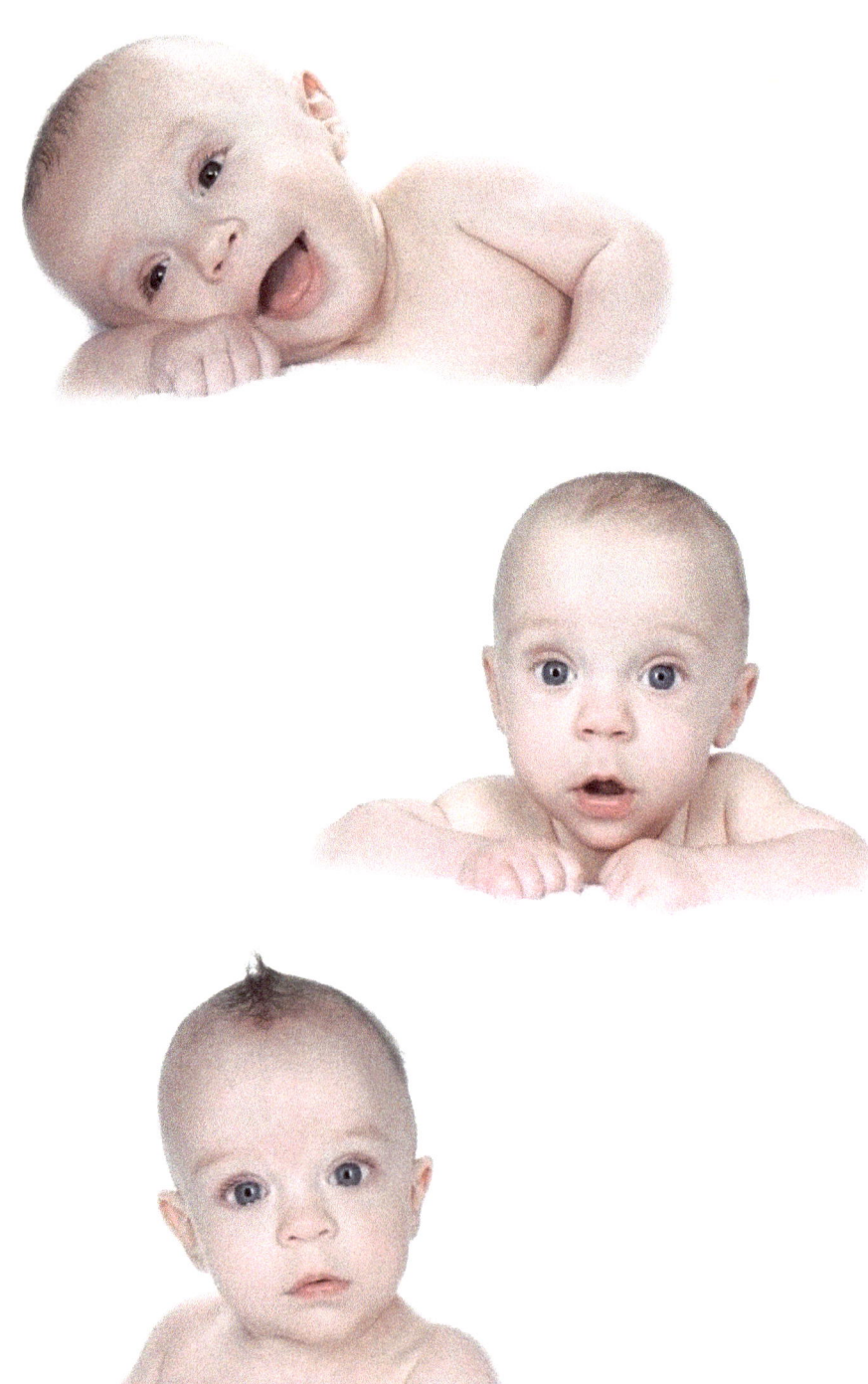

Thee night is far gone; the day is at hand. So then let us cast off the works of darkness and put on the armor of light.

Romans 13:12 (ESV)

Our house was full of guests for the first couple weeks after bringing our babies home. My parents stayed with us for three months to help. My mom would help me out of bed everyday so I could hold my babies. I tried so hard to be a mom but being a mom was too hard on me. By the time my babies were home, I had already become too weak to do anything but stare at them. I wasn't their mom. I was just the dying girl in the back room. Too fatigued to walk, talk or stand. Too weak to care for my babies and too weak to care for myself.

Every night I imagined getting out of bed and feeding my babies. Changing their diapers and giving them baths. Holding them in warm blanket to show my love and a large crowd to share my joy. I dreamt for this day. Every day.

After three months, my mom and dad were exhausted and decided it would be best if they took Dominic home with them, since he was so colicky. It was as if they had already pre-planned this and the effects it would have on me were not even a concern. I fell on the floor begging her not to take him. I cried so hard it felt like my heart was being torn apart. I felt betrayed and lost. It was physically beyond what I was able to endure. I was too weak to fight. All I could do was watch as my life began to fall into darkness. I cried for days as my mind and soul tore my flesh. I fell deeper and deeper into a pit of despair. I finally decided I had to stop loving my son, which was impossible. But the pain of losing him was more than my heart could hold.

My mom would bring Dominic home a couple times a week so I could see him. My mother-in-law, Phyllis and my Aunt Dianna were always there to take care of Jayden and Gavin. I wasn't well enough to care for them on my own. As soon as Brandon left for work each morning, there was always someone there to fill in.

I was seldom alone but the day I was…. I laid Jayden and Gavin in their boppies to watch Sprout. I started to feel powerless and began to text Brandon letters that never formed a word. I began to feel my body shake as I fell to the floor. I laid right next to my babies in convulsions. My sister-in-law and husband sensed that something was wrong. They quickly found me and called the ambulance. The paramedics drugged me with an IV of Ambien and caused the convulsions and my heart rate to increase. I was pronounced dead on arrival but somehow revived. The doctors left me in the ER for hours because they didn't know how to care for me. My mom insisted they call my Endocrinologist. I was told that all Dr. Maruca said was "Cortisone! Adrenal Failure! Cortisone! Get it!" Apparently, it worked because I woke up hours later, cuffed to an ICU bed. During the time I was chained to another bed, I began to develop muscle spasms and sleep paralysis. They were caused by the reaction to the drugs in my IV and years of being bedridden.

I felt overpowered by the fear of sleep paralysis. It attacked me every day. Half asleep and half awake, my body would become paralyzed. I constantly felt the presence of fear as I was unable to open my eyes. I struggled and struggled and fought for strength but would awake again in the same situation. I would fight and fight until I finally broke free and try to stay awake, in fear of experiencing it again. I lived in constant fear with no joy in my life. Exhaustion entangled me and I lost my miracle.

As soon as I was discharged from the hospital, my family decided that I was incapable of caring for two babies. I lost my miracle baby and immediately cursed God. I cursed Him more than I praised Him. I had no one to rely on but people and people let me down. My parents took Jayden home with them because he was on oxygen and needed special care that I was obviously unable to provide. So, I fell to the floor in agony and tears begging them not to take him. I couldn't handle the betrayal. After I watched Jayden struggle to survive every day in NICU, I couldn't wait for the day I could hold him. He has held a special place in my heart. My heart was broken that day, and I never fully recovered. That's when I decided to give up.

Depressed, weak and defeated. Bronzed again but unaware of who burned me. (2 Corinthian 11:3 ESV) I just completely gave up. I didn't know how to swallow the internal loss. I just wanted to die. I guess you could say I gave in to the devil because he took complete advantage of my sorrow and turned my life into hell. As the weeks went by, I was no longer able to get out of bed. I was confined in utter darkness, again.... but his time I had no way out.

My mom would bring Jayden and Dominic home almost every day so I could see them, while my mother-in-law was always there to care for Gavin. Even though Gavin lived at home and the boys were home during the day, I only saw them for a couple minutes. I was too weak to stay awake. Every time I woke up, my boys were older. They started crawling, walking, and talking and I never witnessed one of these miracles. I missed it all. I gave up my soul in hope of dying. In hope the hell would end.... but it had just begun.

Each day grew shorter as the nights grew darker. Images began to appear. I was terrified and naive but smart enough to distract them, so I thought. Now I have a new horrible habit, sleeping with my light on. It worked but only for a short time. The demons outsmarted me. Which was easy to do seeing I had no knowledge of my authority over them. "Behold, I have given you authority to tread on serpents and scorpions, and over all the power of the enemy, and nothing shall hurt you." Luke 10:19 (ESV).

I allowed the enemy in so easily. I am assuming it was my personal sins that opened this gaping hole. But I was unaware as demons planted each and every failure. I could see them as they flew above me like vultures, and I could feel them as they ran to torment me each and every hour. The deep, sharp claws latched to my skin and spun me around the room. I was constantly dizzy. I was tormented all day and all night. I fell deeper and deeper into satan's trap and gradually lost more and more of my life. A year here, a year there. A total of 12.

I would cry out. "God Help Me" but I had no faith to believe. My strength was beyond fatigued and I often collapsed out of weakness. I was unable to carry myself anymore and I lost every inch of muscle mass. I was skin and bones. I fell out of bed every time I tried to get up by myself. I would lay in the same position I fell and scream for someone to hear. But no one could hear me. I could never cry louder than my babies. I was so weak I had no breath to continue screaming, but eventually someone would find me. I wept in agony over what my life had become…. I was stuck in that bed so long that I barely had the strength to survive. All I could do was wait for the day my life and the torture would finally end.

Out of chronic fatigue, I slept 23 hours a day, for 10 years. I prayed every night that I wouldn't wake up. But when I did, all I wanted to do was cry. For twelve years, I cried every single day. As I am now, recalling it.

The sweetest of memories were quickly stollen from me and all I can remember are the pictures. As fatigue became sorrow, sorrow became anger and soon became my only source of life. I knew no other way to survive. I had no armor. I had no protection. I was a target for the fiery darts of the devil without the shield of faith to save me. My soul was strapped to the fire but then I heard His name.

It was 2010 and I was wailing and crying for help while lost in a nightmare. Unable to walk, I would crawl with fear in my head. What have I become? And constantly cry out "God, why did you do this to me?" Every day I was trapped in torture and unable to move. I was too weak to do anything but wait until I never awoke to this nightmare again…but I always did. I cried out again, "God, why won't you just let me die?" I believed my wounds were too deep to heal.

It seems the most tragic experiences are the only ones I remember. I was dying from internal failure and my son Jayden was dying of lung disease. Brandon suddenly felt a strong urge to take us to church. It had been 13 years since I walked into a church to worship God.

I will never forget the first time I stepped foot into Faith Heights Church in Grand Junction, Co. I could barely walk to the sanctuary but by the grace of God, I made it. Bright lights filled the stage, and the music was like nothing I had ever heard. The lyrics on the screen spoke to me and at that moment, I realized God had rescued us. A huge burden was immediately lifted from my heart as I gave my life to Christ.

I looked around and gazed at the congregation praising God. Lifting theirs arms up to God and dancing in circles as they sang Rooftops by Jesus Culture.

"Here I am before You

Falling in love and seeking Your truth

Knowing that Your perfect grace

Has brought me to this place

Because of You I freely live

My life to You, O God, I give

So I stand before You, God

I lift my voice 'cause You set me free"

I had no idea what was going on around me, but I felt the spirits surround me. I had never felt as alive as I did that first day. The first scripture Pastor John Cappetto imprinted in my heart was Mark 11:24 and it was a relief to my mind and soul. "If you believe with all your heart, you can have whatever you ask for".

I tried to believe but I had no idea how to have faith. I didn't know the scriptures that taught authority. I was lied to. Every day and every night satan constantly whispered in my ear, "God doesn't love you!" "Look at everything you've done!" I believed him but I didn't want to. I wanted to believe that God loved me and wanted me well. But I didn't have enough faith in the scriptures that say so. I cried out to God, and he gave me Isaiah 41:10 (ESV), "Fear not for I am with you; be not dismayed for I am your God; I will strengthen you; I will help you; I will uphold you with my righteous right hand."

After a couple months of attending church, our pastor invited a healer, Pastor Dave Duell from Lakewood, Co. I could feel a presence as we stepped inside the sanctuary. I thought I was looking at God as the powerful light, shining around him, dropped us to the floor. I was a baby Christian at the time. Learning how to walk in the right direction. Learning how to trust in God and the power in his word. The Lord brought us back to church right on time. Right on time to save Jayden's life and right on time to save mine. I believe it was our faith that saved our son's life that night.

As Pastor Dave began to lay hands on the congregation, I stepped out in faith to be healed. As soon as his hands touched my head, I felt an electrical shock throughout my body as I fell to the floor. I had never felt anything like that before. I had only heard of it. In excitement and fear of losing my son, I "ran" up the stairs and grabbed Jayden from the nursery. He was only 3 at the time. Pastor Dave asked me what Jayden needed healing from. I said, "Chronic Lung Disease". He repeated my every word as he laid hands on his lungs. Jayden's eyes rolled back in his head as he began to fall. The ushers stood behind to catch him. I looked at the congregation with open mouths and speechless voices as they witnessed the mercy of God. Jayden's lungs were instantly healed as God erased Chronic Lung Disease from his charts. Though I did not receive healing that night, my son did. Because of past sins and failures, I didn't have faith in the power of God to heal me. But I did have faith in the power of God to heal my son. My heart was cleansed that night, as I reached another step.

Even though I was climbing the ladder of faith, I was still bound with fear. Afraid of the dark. Afraid of my own shadow, and every creeping thing that creepeth upon the earth…or in my room at night. As if the fallen angels who joined satan were freed from the pit of the earth just to lurk around and await a chance to devour me. I know Jesus brought me to Faith Heights Church to deliver me from oppression.

Soon after joining our new church, Pastor Mark Hankins and his wife Trina visited our church for a Holy Ghost Meeting. They called for anyone who hadn't been filled with the Holy Spirit to speak in tongues to come up to be filled. I didn't hesitate to come forward. I think Pastor Hankins and his wife spent ten to fifteen minutes trying to clear out years of sickness and fear, heartache and pain. I cried the entire time as the Holy Spirit cast out darkness. I may not have spoken in tongues that night, but my tears turned to laughter as the comforter took his place. I laughed for hours. Jayden was in the nursery, and I was still laughing when we took him home. My laughter caused Jayden to laugh, and we laughed all through the night in total serenity. Not only was I filled with laughter, but the Holy Spirit also filled me with peace. Peace over fear. I slept that night for the first time in a decade with no fear. The Holy Spirit was with me as I walked through my room in the dark. Not one creeping thing touched me, and they haven't since.

After a couple months of hearing the scriptures that promise healing, I was ready to receive for myself. I told Pastor John, "I'm sick of being sick". So, I stopped taking all my mediations and claimed I was healed then and there. It was amazing how much healthier I was when I relied on God instead of medications to keep me alive. I was doing so well holding on to my faith. I was determined not to let go. My endocrinologist took one look at me and began to shake his head. He sat there for what seemed like forever trying to contemplate how I was still alive. I had missed 2 months of medications that "kept me alive". My doctor was stressed but all I could do was keep pointing up.

My faith was stronger than ever. I was enjoying my life again. I was a mom, and my babies were finally home. Though I was doing so well, my family was scared. They assumed my pastor encouraged me to stop taking all my medications, which he never did. I made that decision on my own. They would point out that I was retaining water, and something wasn't right. I heard it so much I began to feel their fear and I lost faith in my healing. I immediately had to go back on all my medications. Another "I guess He doesn't want me healed".

Here I am again, for the fourth time, bedridden and sick. How am I going to get myself out of this now? Well, I didn't. Not for another eight years. I never stopped attending church. I attended 2-3 times a week. But no matter how full I was of the word, the doubt remained and every attempt to receive healing turned to disappointment. Unable to maintain faith and full of doubt. I was back to darkness but this time I wasn't alone.

The Galleria

The Galleria

Chapter Five
Lack of Knowledge

I've lived through many storms. A few flew past me but most of them defeated me. All because of my lack of knowledge in the Word.

"My people are destroyed for lack of knowledge; because you have rejected knowledge, I reject you from being a priest to me. And since you have forgotten the law of your God, I also will forget your children." Hosea 4:6 (ESV).

This story of my life is a taste of reality. A true testimony of what life is like without God. To be alone is to live in darkness as without hope is to be hopeless. People pray in hell, but no one answers.

Exodus 23:25 (ESV) says, "You shall serve the Lord your God, and he will bless your bread and your water, and I will take sickness away from among you". This scripture would have saved me in the beginning, but I never took authority over my life. I never educated myself in the truth and life that the Word of God teaches. To tell you the truth, I didn't know how. I didn't even know where to begin.

As a result of ignorance, I lived decades in sickness, sin and defeat. Believing my life was spared just to be a lesson for others. The lies entangled me as I fell for every word that came from their unscriptural mouths.

I was stuck and I didn't know how to get out. But after years and years of being tormented, I finally listened to the rusty voice in the background. I tore through the spirit of lies and opened the pages of truth.

For so many years I thought God wanted me to be sick so "I could be a lesson to others." That's what I was always told. I had decided I didn't want to serve a God who would allow the devil to destroy my life to teach someone else a lesson. So, for over ten years I stopped serving Him. That's why my life fell apart.

Let's back up... I met my husband, Brandon, 3 years after graduating from high school. We were such a perfect couple we married shortly after. Our first 5 years were a blast. We were making a ton of money, buying and selling houses, going on trips and my husband was touring in a band! Good times....and then all the sudden I was bedridden, and the doctors had no cure.... I went all over the United States looking for a second opinion but was only left to face another disappointment. My mom flew me all the way to Nashville, Tennessee to see one of the "best" Endocrinologist. After observing my MRI, the doctor said, "That's amazing". My mom and I were excited. Finally! Someone had the answer! Then the doctor said, "Well not amazing for you, I've never seen a pituitary stem completely depleted". It was like a sharp knife through my heart. According to this doctor, there was nothing he could do for me. I would just have to spend the rest of my life sick until I died.

Trying to function as a sick person just didn't work for me. I failed at everything I tried to accomplish. The physical weakness was more than I could bear. Thoughts of suicide began to circle around my brain. Satan would whisper in my ear, "Life's over for you just kill yourself and end your suffering." Out of ignorance, I thought that was God talking to me. I would start to think of how I was going to kill myself and instantly become strong enough to reach over on that nightstand and swallow a bottle of pills. The overdose would paralyze me but eventually someone would find the empty bottle. I always hoped they'd save me too late so I could die but they always found me right on time.

The years passed and I moved on from the idea of ending my life and decided to create life instead. I truly believed that having a baby would fix everything in my life. I would have been such a good mom.

12 years ago, I made an honorable decision and I've been paying for it ever since....

What if I had educated myself in the Word? What would my life have been like. Not bedridden and sick 24/7. Every single day for 12 years. Giving life to a child is supposed to be the beginning of a new and better life, filled with joyful memories. But for me, it was only a loss. That's all I felt. I was too sick to get out of bed. So, I never got to hold them and play with them or change their diapers and feed them or teach them and laugh when they made cute noises or cry out of happiness. No, I just cried, and I still haven't stopped.

I cry because of the loss in my life and the pain in my heart. I feel this all the time. All because I was ignorant of the Word of God. It's been 12 years, and I don't remember a day.

I don't remember because I was drugged, sick and hopeless. I had no faith.... but most of all, I didn't have the energy to read the Word. For all those years, I never educated myself. I had no knowledge, no faith and no strength to learn how to. I didn't learn how to have faith until I felt well enough to read the scriptures that promise it. I would not have learned the truth, nor would I have lived to tell it without medical cannabis.

I've had conversations with God about taking CBC and cannabis. I talked to Him about taking the earth's medicine. I asked Him "Dear God, I don't know how to get out of bed without it." I would ask Him "I don't understand. Is this a sin?" His answer was always comfort and I knew he understood. He walks with me and sometimes for me. He is my strength. Sativa is a temporary replacement. It's a boost of serotonin that gives me the physical strength to rise from that bed of sickness. One dose and God leads me the rest of the day. It is the only medicine that constantly gives me natural energy. Here's the od part, it's the only medication I've ever taken that gives me the stamina to read the Word of God. It's the only medication I've ever taken that gives me the mental strength to keep reaching for a goal, knowledge.

"For the Lord gives wisdom; from his mouth comes knowledge and understanding." Proverbs 2:6 (ESV).

Chapter Six
Break the Chains

www.GALLERIAGJ.com

55

I wanted to be a vessel, I wanted to save everyone. To preach the gospel of Jesus Christ. To heal and save…but I couldn't even heal myself. I was lost in the fiery darts of the devil, and I could barely breathe. I had no other choice. I had to learn how to throw them back. I had to learn how to take back my life, my husband and my babies.

Did you know that you have the power of God to cast evil spirits back to hell? Every morning when I awake, I claim "I'm redeemed by the blood of Jesus, Healed by His Stripes and NO POWER can come against me!" This was one of the most powerful weapons I learned from Pastor Mark Hankins, the power in my words. I say this over and over until I believe it. My faith is strong when I claim these words and I have the power of God to get out of bed and live and prosper. I no longer fear the devil. He fears me! "Even though I walk through the valley of the shadow of death, I will fear no evil, for you are with me, your rod and your staff, they comfort me." Psalm 23:4 (ESV).

I stood my ground and claimed the Word. The Word is knowledge, its power, but you can only use this power with faith.

I will never forget the first time I stepped in a faith-based church. Ten years prior, I was avoiding church and cursing God. That first day back… I was amazed by the music and Word. It was a relief to my mind and soul. I heard Mark 11:24 for the first time. If you read it and say it, you will believe it and you will have whatever you ask for.

I stopped taking all my medications and claimed, "I'm healed." I went two months without the medications that "kept me alive" because my faith was strong in God's Word. My endocrinologist was astonished. He sat in his chair with his eyes shut trying to contemplate how this was even possible. I said, "It's God".

Wow my faith was so strong. I had no doubt in my mind that I was healed. But my family started getting worried. They began to point out that I was retaining water and that I looked tired and flushed. I heard it so much I began to feel defeated by their fear. I lost my faith and my healing all because I lost faith in the healing power of God. The result, I'm fighting off demons again. Bedridden and struggling to regain faith. How did I allow the devil back in?

The devil had power over me. He attached to my skin and never let go. Every time I would say "In the name of Lord Jesus, I command you to leave and go back to hell where you came from." The demons would disappear for about five minutes but would always return to torture me.

I was bound with shackles and chains. If only I had claimed the Word. If you speak the Word and claim these scriptures, this evil will no longer have any place in your life." Death and life are in the power of the tongue….." Proverbs 18:21 (ESV). Your faith will grow, and you will say "I Am Righteous"! "Evil has no hold on me!

As one of many who have experienced the hell life can bring us, I have been through more than anyone should ever have to go through in a lifetime. Psalm 34:19 (ESV), says, "Many are the afflictions of the righteous, but the Lord delivers him out of them all."

As I laid sick in bed for over a decade, I never realized how much valuable time I had lost. So, I began to take in anything I could find to mask the pain. Everything but the Word. And the day I finally walked out of that bed…it was like I woke up to a new life but in reality, a nightmare.

It's a choice. Am I going to wake up and be consumed by the storm or am I going to be the storm. Proverbs 17:22 (ESV), says "A joyful heart is good medicine, but a crushed spirit dries up the bones". So, it's up to me. It's up to you. We have a choice. We must change our mindset. I can no longer look to the past to define me. I'm looking to God. For only He can judge me. "There is only one lawgiver and judge, he who is able to save and to destroy. But who are you to judge your neighbor?" James 4:12 (ESV).

After years of attending service at church, I realized my faith wasn't strong enough to receive. I had hands laid on me so many times I can't even count. Every healing line turned out the same. I would walk up, receive and then automatically lose it. For a day or so I would think, "I still feel the same but I'm going to continue to believe" and then, like so many trying to receive, I would realize I still felt sick and say, "I guess God doesn't want me healed". That was a lie from the devil, but I didn't know how to be set free from the constant curse of unbelief. I began to realize that I needed to know more about the Word to be healed. I needed to understand my authority. I needed to know the truth. I needed to know the word to have faith in it. So, I prayed, and He instantly answered me. It only took that one prayer for God to bring bible college to my mind. The more God spoke to me, the more eager I became. One day I felt an urgency to call my church to talk to them about what God said. I started my first class at Rhema Bible College a couple weeks later. It felt like God was unraveling the lost pieces to the puzzle. The millions of pieces to the puzzle of my life. The first book arrived, and I tore into it with excitement. I sat and stared in a daze as I imagined a new beginning.

In my first semester, I learned what it really means to have faith in God. Hebrews 11:1 (ISV), tells us what faith is, "Now faith is the assurance that what we hope for will come about and the certainty that what we cannot see exists." Roman 10:17 (NKJV), tells us how to get it. "Faith comes by hearing and hearing by the Word of God". Reading these scriptures every day gave me more than hope. The words constantly ran through my mind. Scripture after scripture circling in my heart. After a couple weeks of studying, my faith became strong enough to receive whatever I asked for. I was doing so well. God's word gave me the energy to get up every morning and take my boys to school. I would spend all day reading books about faith and healing. I was so absorbed with the truth in the Word of God that nothing could break me. I was healed. I could feel it. I was even exercising every day and taking care of my family. I felt so healthy. My life was turning around. I was finally back on track.

For days I heard a voice telling me I was well enough to work. I felt a huge burden laid upon me and a sense of urgency to find a job. How did I not see it coming. The pressure was weighing on me and I never stopped to realize that this wasn't God at all. How easily I was led astray. How easily the serpent slithered in to swallow me whole again. I was led away from everything and everyone I ever wanted. I lost 3 more years of my children's lives….3 more years of my life….3 more years out of touch with God. I was so busy working I barely had time to read my books, let alone the bible. Oh man! I was fooled again. 2 Corinthians 11:14 (ESV), Paul writes, "…Satan disguises himself as an angel of light". The devil didn't want me healed so he did whatever he could to stop it.

1 Peter 5:8 (NIV)…" your enemy the devil prowls around like a roaring lion looking for someone to devour".

After I started working again, I immediately became ill. Really ill. My PCP diagnosed me with Addison's Disease, autoimmune deficiency. This "new" diagnosis explained every major symptom I was suffering with. But my endocrinologist never diagnosed me with this disease. Years after he passed away, a new endocrinologist told me it was because my actual diagnosis is panhypopituitarism and it is much worse than Addison's Disease. But I've never met a doctor who understood what panhypopituitarism is. Every time I went to the emergency room, I would be left on IV's and oxygen and not one doctor had a clue as to what to do for me. But if I say "Addison's Disease" they instantly inject me with cortisol.

Immediately after being diagnosed with an understanding of adrenal failure, I started to get sick at every job. I was sent to the ER so many times I was starting to owe more money on medical bills than I was making. The doctors would give me a huge dose of cortisone, corticosteroids, to strengthen my immunity to fight off every virus that attacked me. I realized that I was not healthy enough to have a career

I thought, why did I stop my bible study to work? What did I just do to myself? Did I seriously just allow the devil to deceive me AGAIN? 2 Corinthians 11:3 says, (NIV) "……just as Eve was deceived by the serpent's cunning, your minds may somehow be led astray for your sincere and pure devotion to Christ". I just wasted another 3 years because I thought it was God's plan for me to go back to work. It was just another scheme from the devil and now I know why. He's afraid. He's afraid of me being healed. He's afraid of you being healed. He's afraid because he will lose the power, he has had over us for so long. So, I believe I have a responsibility now. I have to make up for the time I've lost.

Now I'm spending every day trying to get back to that place. That perfect state of peace, confidence and security. John 16:33 (NIV) says, "I have told you these things, so that in me you may have peace…." That perfect peace. Isaiah 26:3 (DBY), "Thou wilt keep in perfect peace the mind stayed (on thee), for he confideth in thee".

So, the more I write, the more I tell you my story, the stronger I become in the spirit and in peace. You are here with me right now. In my mind and in my heart. For the rest of this book, you will be a witness of healing. I'm testifying to you that I will maintain my faith to lift yours.

When I look back at how God designed my life and marked my paths, I see that in everything I've gone through, there's always a lesson to learn. Perhaps it was God's plan for me to go back to work…or maybe, he made the best out of my decision. Romans 8:28 (NIV) says, …And we know that in all things God works for the good of those who love him, who have been called according to his purpose.

Now, I can honestly say, my first job back to work wasn't the job I wanted but it got me to the job I needed. Newly diagnosed and still unaware of the depth of sickness I opened the door to just by going back into the world. I worked at a plasma center where hundreds of people would come in and out of the donor center to donate plasma. Even with a face shield on, I constantly became ill. So ill that I was rushed to the ER every time. Still striving toward ministry in my future, I ministered to the donors and to the fellow employees. Some listened but many turned their ears from me. Did they not realize the miracle that was standing in front of them? How could they? All they ever witnessed was the aftermath. Working with people who seemed my age yet some-how they were young enough to be my children. The look on their faces when I told them my real age. Jaws dropped with disbelief. If they only knew; I have the same face every day when I look in the mirror. To you I look a lot younger than I am, yet I feel younger than I look.

[My mom has always looked 10—15 years younger than she is. She is the most beautiful woman I have ever seen. My boyfriends would always flirt with her. That was kind of embarrassing, then. I notice now that a lot of women mistreated my mom when I was younger. Now I get it. Jealousy. Isn't that an ugly word? James 3:16 (AMP) says, "For where jealousy and selfish ambition exist, there is disorder [unrest, rebellion] and every evil thing and morally degrading practice."]

How to explain being extinct from the world for 12 years and then going back to work…here I am learning a new language again. This time I didn't get a speech therapist, though one would have been convenient. Here I go again, trying to talk to people from a different planet. I hear "that was like a minute ago" and I'm like "What? That was like 10 years ago!" I was a blast from the past. It seems I was quite a laugh. One day I said "burn" and a co-worker said "dang, you have been gone a long time". Ya, thanks for the reminder. It was so similar to my walk back into high school. But this time they weren't laughing at me. They were laughing with me, I think.

So, off to God's next plan. I was curious to see what He has under his miraculous sleeves. A couple weeks later I received a call from seriously, the coolest person I've ever met; Moneda. We shared many interests related to work ethics and Christian beliefs. I've never had a boss as awesome as this girl. She hired me on as a paramedical examiner to travel all over for health fairs and insurance examines. This was my chance to grow up. No one to take care of me, or as Dr. Maruca would say, "enable me". I had to learn how to take care of myself. It was the first time I had ever driven a long distance by myself. The first time I ever ate by myself of stayed at a hotel by myself, well, doing anything by myself for that matter!

I traveled to Moneda's office at Quest Diagnostics in Colorado Springs, Co, a couple times a month and would stay a week to work in her lab. The most memorable trip we took together was when I drove 7 hours in the snow to pick her up at her office. We then drove, I don't even know how many hours, to Trinidad, Co. It was the first spiritual battle we faced together. We pulled up to a fancy Laquinta on the border of New Mexico. I didn't understand the irony in that until we walked through the sliding doors. I said, "Did you feel that" and she said in a startled voice, "Ya". We rebuked that spirit and walked to the receptionist. To our surprise, not only did the employees seem clueless about the demonic power flowing through the building, but all their faces also looked like clay. To tell you the truth, everyone in that hotel looked like clay. We thought we were in a twilight zone surrounded by aliens, well, demons, same difference.

The most significant part of the story is when we took our authority and claimed the blood of Jesus over the entire hotel. We cast out darkness and welcomed the Holy Spirit, Host and Angels. We each had our own big fancy room down the hall from each other. Wearing our armor and full of supernatural strength. We had no fear and slept straight through the night. Always in the back of my head and full in the spirit, "For God has not given us a spirit of fear but of power and love a sound mind." 2 Timothy 1:7 (NKJV). I met Moneda downstairs for breakfast at 0530 in the morning and to our surprise, though God never ceases to amaze me, everyone looked human again.

It was an amazing experience to work for someone you admired. But like so many scenarios in my life, this one also ended in illness. (If I had a choice I would have never left. But then again, if I hadn't you wouldn't be reading my testimony.) Besides the time I was spending away from my family, my health was declining from exhaustion. My last working trip ended when an ambulance was called to Quest Diagnostics in Colorado Springs, Co. I had stepped away from the lab to get a breath but was found a couple minutes later, on the floor. Breathing but unresponsive. When I awoke in the ER Moneda was right there by my side. Wow. My own boss went in the ambulance with me. It was obvious that this position was ordained by God. I not only learned my position by the best trainer but even more, Moneda taught me how to truly fight the good fight of faith.

Off to another new beginning. If only I had known, it was the beginning of the end. Finally, back to a hospital position…but something was missing…or full of something I hate. Every single time I opened the door to this medical laboratory, I opened another door to a demonic atmosphere. Why in the world would God put me in an atheist, scientology department? Talk about not fitting in, again. As I was the only Christian in that specific field. I was not allowed to talk about my beliefs, only theirs. Almost three months of this and I constantly asked God, WHY? I don't remember how many times I threw my badge down and said, "I quit". I walked out of the laboratory almost every time, and rwould

63

then remember I had to have my badge to get out of the hospital. Again, I don't remember how many times I had to knock on the door to the lab. I always got the same look as they handed me my badge. I wanted to leave so bad, but God kept saying "Not Yet", "Not Yet"! So, I listened and I'm so thankful I did. It was mid-March when Covid hit Grand Junction, Co. Can you imagine the hysteria it caused in a Godless laboratory? Everyone is freaking out and deep down inside, I'm laughing because God did not give us a spirit of fear but of power and love and a sound mind. (See 2 Timothy 1:7) But only someone who follows Christ would understand that. Somehow, I knew this was going to happen. In fall of 2019 I had a vision that something was going to hit the world hard, and its main purpose was to separate us all. I kept it to myself until Christmas Eve 2019 when the Holy Spirit gave me utterance to tell everyone at the party that a virus was coming, and this was our last Christmas together. Of course, they smirked at me and laughed or possibly thought I was high. Lol. So, when it finally hit, instead of feeling any sense of fear, I thought, yay. Now my family will stop assuming my mind's just full of weed. No, I'm just high on God!

Once this man-made virus hit the hospitals, my PCP contacted my employer. I was sent home due to my diagnosis of "Addison's Disease", immune deficiency. See what happens when you listen to God? I didn't even have to quit. Not only was I relieved from that pit of Hell, I also received the willpower to write my testimony.

I was overzealous by the mercy of God. What would have happened if I had listened to my flesh instead of the Holy Spirit? He was with me the entire time. He gave me supernatural strength to fight the "natural". Strength to stand and keep standing. He directed my path to victory. I would have truly been lost without him. I would have fallen apart when the girls in the lab made fun of the scars on my neck. When they laughed and whispered, "She's probably suicidal." I would have fallen when they

64

belittled me, talked down to me and made fun of my beliefs. I would have fallen if I hadn't paid attention to that still, small voice that said, "Fear not, for I am with you; be not dismayed, for I am your God; I will strengthen you, I will help you, I will uphold you with my righteous right hand." Isaiah 41:10 ESV.

I believe it was July 1st, 2021, when I emailed my finalized manuscript to my first publisher, Trinity Broadcast Network. I had prayed and prayed to God about publishing my story with TBN. I saw an ad a couple days later on Facebook. I sent the only 4 chapters I had written. A couple weeks later, I received a call from a publisher at TBN telling me that they were interested in publishing my testimony and would give me a year to complete it. I thought to myself, wow, a whole year. I could write a novel with that much time. Ya, that didn't happen. You would think that when you're called to fulfill an assignment from God, He would make sure it would go smoothly for you. I'm sure that was His plan but satan rocked my path. In September of 2020, a couple months into writing my full testimony, I lifted a box that was too heavy for me. I felt it like sciatica instantly. I went to my bed to lay down and pop my back in place. Oh, the agony. Out of all the physical pain I have ever endured, this was by far, the worst. I cried and screamed immediately after I heard a crack. I was automatically bent completely over to my knees. I could no longer stand up straight. Of course, it was a weekend! I had never felt anything like this before. I was in shock and honestly, a little afraid. Fear of extreme pain. Fear of permanent handicap. Fear I just lost everything I was published to accomplish.

For 6 months I was semi-restrained to my bed. It would have been constant but thankfully I had a friend who needed me. Thankful…because if she hadn't needed me…if God hadn't entrusted me with this expectation, my entire life would have been focused on myself. Over the physical pain and mental anguish. But God gave me this responsibility to strengthen me. I imagine the assignments Jesus gave his disciples. To go out and preach the word to every creature. (See Mark 16:15). The trials and tribulations set before them. They wouldn't back down because they put all their trust in their savior. Yes, a couple fell, but don't we all? On the day of Passover, Peter denied knowing Jesus, three times in Matthew 26:74. Then in Matthew 26:75 (NIV), Peter remembered the words Jesus had spoken: "Before the rooster crows, you will deny me three times." And he went outside and wept bitterly.

As an example, and testament to us, Peter brushed off his failures and continued to share the gospel. A story of a deep love for Jesus Christ. Without His love and forgiveness, there really is no other way to move on from our falls and failures. And we all know what Judas did. We gasp and say, "I would NEVER" and completely condemn him for betraying Christ. I think a lot of us need to take a better look at ourselves when we consider his actions. Who are we to judge? Romans 14:4 (NIV) says, "Who are you to judge someone else's servant? To their own master, servants stand or fall. And they will stand, for the Lord is able to make them stand."

Free of judgment, I continued as a servant of Christ to put the needs of others above my own. Honestly, it's a lot easier when it's someone you cherish.

1 Peter 1:7-9 (TLB) says, "These trials are only to test your faith, to see whether or not it is strong and pure. It is being tested as fire tests gold and purifies it and your faith is far more precious to God than mere gold; if your faith remains strong after being tried in the test tube of fiery trials, it will bring you much praise and glory and honor on the day of his return. You love him even though you have never seen him; though not seeing him, you trust him; and even now you are happy with the inexpressible joy that comes from heaven itself. And your further reward for trusting him will be the salvation of your souls."

Unfortunately, by the 4th month, I had lost the ability to help anyone, especially myself. A couple trips to the chiropractor and constantly being told "it's just really bad sciatica" … "It's just more painful to you because of your low cortisol levels". The unexplainable diagnosis. I couldn't take it anymore. I couldn't walk or sit or lay down. Every time I tried to get in a car, I had to jump out at least ten times trying to realign my "back". I slept on my back with my arms under my knees and raised up to my chest! The pain was so intense, I hadn't written anything for 5 months. I had to find a second opinion. I remember when I was finally referred to a pain specialist. I was bound to a wheelchair. Deep lines began to form around my face from expressions of torment. It was on a Thursday that my mom wheeled me in to finally get relief, but the man at the front desk said, "Ok, we can get you in next Monday". I started balling as my mom wheeled me out of the office. I cried out, loudly, "No please I can't take 3 more days!" With empathy, thank God, the receptionist rescheduled me for the next day. I counted the seconds until my next appointment, imagining the freedom. Over the course of 2 months, I received 3 steroid injections like an epidural. The first two failed until they finally did an MRI and found out it wasn't my back out of place…it was my hip! Over the past 6 months it had turned into a herniated disc. The pain specialist seemed amazed with my ability to sustain such intense pain for so long. Sustain? I wanted to bang my head against the wall to pass out from the pain. Sustain! Lol. I wonder, why did this particular trial take so long to unravel? Was it a successful attempt for satan to take more time from my life or a failed attempt to stop me from publishing my testimony?

The 3rd cortisone injection was my last for this diagnosis. The pain specialists continued to call me on a regular basis wondering why I didn't need another shot. They had told me that I could get one more injection but after that it was surgery. That was over 3 years ago. Now my hip is back in place and no herniated disc. "How is that possible" the doctors ask. Lol. "All things are possible to them who believe." (See Philippians

4:13). Another lesson learned and another terminated trial. No more pain. Able to walk. Able to write again, so I thought. Here comes the next attack to try and stop me. It was late March in 2021 and I was on my 6th chapter, reaching for 12.

The fear of Covid had gone rampage over Grand Junction, Co. Everyone covered in masks…or trash bags…or any other household item to bring us humor. For so long I thought, "this is a stupid man-made virus made by Satan and it will only attack those naive of their authority in Christ". So, our bible study continued to meet every Saturday and Sunday. We learned our redemptive gifts and how to fight spiritual warfare. Was it the gathering that caused us all to get sick or perhaps it was another attack from the enemy to stop us from learning how to defeat the battles he was throwing at us. The demonic power was heavy as demons pushed some of us to the floor. Maybe we stepped too far into the truth. Too far into another world. Maybe we knew too much. Whatever the reason, we all felt the consequence. I have to say, with immune deficiency you never know what awkwardly awful symptoms you're going to endure. Though my husband recovered within a month, it took me three. For the first month I was so fatigued I could barely open my eyes and move. Crawling to the bathroom again. Barely an appetite but other than nausea, what good would it do to eat, I couldn't taste anything…I couldn't even smell anything…and I had an awful taste in my mouth for 2 months. Everything tasted metallic, like I was full of man-made chemicals. Trying to communicate with God but I was too weak to talk, read or think. Trying to communicate with my church for support but so blind I couldn't read their replies. By the third month I began to see symptoms clear as others appeared. One foot grew longer than the other, my whole body broke out in what looked like a million bug bites, but they didn't itch. Honestly, I couldn't feel them at all. The aftereffects of this virus left, what seem like, long term effects. My vision changed from -.75 to -2.75 in both eyes. The memory loss was significant, though I see it's getting better. As this tragic event has changed many of our lives, I am still expectant of full recovery for every one of us who suffered the effects of Covid 19. But I must add, if it hadn't been for Medical Marijuana, I would have been in the hospital fighting for my life. The truth came out months later that cannabis was a cure for Covid.

Nine months lost to trials and only three left to write my testimony. By contract, my manuscript was due July 1, 2021. Not a day later. For the time I was given, I wrote my entire testimony…with some missing pieces. By the mercy of God, I've been given a second chance to fill in the gaps.

If you look back at your life now, after everything you've endured, everything you've overcome, you realize how much you've learned. And if you look deep enough into your story, God will open your eyes to see Him as He fights your battles. He will remind you of all the times He saved your life. Once you open your heart and mind to that possibility, the road to your future is painted in the blood of Jesus.

I will no longer fear the storms that come my way. I have the power of faith in my voice. I count the joy in every battle because every battle brings me closer to God. With faith I lift my voice and claim the word over every affliction. With faith I will rest in peace as God fights my every battle… "but with us is the Lord our God, to help us and to fight our battles." 2 Chronicles 32:8 (NIV). That means, every time we face a battle, God will be right there fighting it for us. Have you ever wondered why you go through so many storms? Would you believe me if I told you? It's simply because we have fallen short of the glory of God. So why do we go through storms? Romans 3:23 (NIV) says, "For all have sinned and fall short of the glory of God". Because of sin, because of temptation…because God is not the god of this world. Satan is. 2 Corinthians 4:4 (NLT), "Satan, who is the god of this world, has blinded the minds of those who don't believe…."

Everything that's wrong with your life was caused by sin. The bible says the only thing we must do to get to heaven is believe that Jesus is the son of God. John 3:16 (ESV), "For God so loved the world, that he gave his only Son, that whoever believes in him should not perish but have eternal life". So, all you must do to have an immortal, eternal life, is to believe. I don't understand, now, how someone could choose between, maybe there's hell but I'll find out when I die, or I could live a joyful, everlasting life but I'd rather sin. Everyone has only one life in which to determine their destiny…. (See Hebrews 9:27, NIV).

Heaven or hell is determined by whether a person believes (puts their trust) in Christ alone to save themselves. So why take that chance? Wouldn't it just be easier to believe? 1 Timothy 4:10 (NIV), says, "That is why we labor and strive, because we have put our hope in the living God, who is the Savior of all people, and especially of those who believe". I've come to realize that most non-believers chose this way of thinking out of pride. They don't want to admit they're wrong. (See 1 John 2:16).

To believe is to be certain that you will receive whatever you ask for. I fought for 27 years to learn my authority over darkness. Now I know the truth. Now I have the faith. Now I have the power to break every chain.

Update:

When I first wrote my testimony, I was under the impression that my previous diagnosis's where incorrect and my real diagnosis was Addison's Disease. I lost my endocrinologist, Joseph Maruca, to cancer in 2017. Recently, God provided me with an endocrinologist I can finally approve of. Someone Dr Maruca would even approve of. It's been six years since I was misdiagnosed, and I never really believed them. My actual diagnosis is Panhypopituitarism. I was confused the entire time I was being treated for Addison's Disease. Addison's is related specifically to adrenal glands. So, I was left to wonder how all my other symptoms fit into this new diagnosis. It never made sense, and it took me 3 years to find an endocrinologist who agreed with me. I only had my PCP to rely on. Even though he misdiagnosed me, he was the only PCP I've ever had that knew exactly how to help me when I became ill from immune deficiency. Dr Maruca diagnosed me with panhypopituitarism the first day he examined me as a brain injured teen. It was around 2001 when he started increasing my Synthroid to increase my energy. It was believed back then that raising your thyroid would give you more energy.

After 30 years of increasing my Synthroid for energy, my new endocrinologist just shared recent studies with me. They found out that increasing your thyroid doesn't give you more energy, it gives you more fatigue. She apologized saying that "the medical field has failed you". Wait a minute…wait a minute. I just spent almost 15 years bedridden with severe tachycardia because my thyroid was TOO HIGH? I missed out on the first 15 years of my boys' lives because I was overmedicated? I have no words to express the disappointment I feel right now. Like so many scenarios in my life. I'm just expected to suck it up and move on. But only God can give me the strength to recover from this loss.

My endocrinologist then explained to me that I am a very rare case. Most people with pituitary deficiency don't struggle with all these added deficiencies. Panhypopituitarism is so rare that scientists have chosen to refrain from exploring any solutions to enhance the lives of anyone with this condition.

My endocrinologist just lowered my Synthroid from 175 mcg to 100 mcg. My heart rate has decreased from 96 bpm to 64 bpm. Though I definitely don't feel strength like the Hulk or speed like the Flash, I am gradually becoming stronger and faster.

I don't believe God planned this. I don't believe God wanted me to suffer at all. But human error played a huge role in all of it. I asked God, was this a test? He said, "No. But now it's a Testimony.

When I'm afraid of more heartache, Jesus reminds me that He is my comforter. I can't live without the word of God. I can't live without the word of faith.

Chapter Seven
The Lord that Heals

D id you know that there is no sickness, disease, pain, or disorder too powerful for God? "I am the LORD, the God of all the peoples of the world. Is anything too hard for me"? Jeremiah 32:27 (NLT). If you've tried to receive His glorious healing and failed multiple times, like me, I can tell you why. But first you must know that to know God we need to seek Him First. Matthew 6:33 (ESV) says "But seek first the kingdom of God and his righteousness, and all these things will be added to you".

1 John 5:14 (NIV) says, "This is the confidence we have in approaching God: that if we ask anything according to his will, he hears us". So why would we doubt His Word? James 1:6 (ESV) says, "But let him ask in faith, with no doubting, for the one who doubts is like a wave of the sea, blown and tossed by the wind, that person should not expect anything from the Lord". How do we surpass this doubt, and build a relationship with God? Proverbs 3:5-8 (ESV), explains this perfectly, "Trust in the Lord with all your heart, and do not lean on your own understanding. In all your ways acknowledge him, and he will make straight your paths. Be not wise in your own eyes; fear the Lord and turn away from evil. It will be healing to your flesh and refreshment to your bones".

After we've built a solid relationship with God, our faith, hope and love will circum. He will make our paths straight. (See Proverbs 3:6 ESV). Meditate on these scriptures. Claim them and say them over and over. Meditate on the Word. Joshua 1:8 (KJV), says, "This book of the law shall not depart out of thy mouth; but thou shalt meditate therein day and night...."

We must be especially careful what we're claiming every day. "Death and life are in the power of the tongue…" Proverbs 18:21 (KJV). On the days that I would awake, the first thing I would usually do is claim that I was ill, bedridden and defeated and all I wanted to do is die. But now I have the knowledge. I am no longer defeated. My faith is in the written word. The Bible says to educate yourself in the word and "…resist the devil and he will flee from you. James 4:7 (NIV). Take a stand. Hold on to your authority.

You have the power. Luke 1:19 (KJV), "Behold, I give unto you power to tread on serpents and scorpions, and over all the power of the enemy: and nothing shall by any means hurt you." Jesus has already won. The struggle is over and it's time to bow down. When you bow down to Christ, your life and health are no longer in the hands of agony. Your life and health are in the healing hands of Christ.

Healing is manifested throughout the entire bible, from the beginning of the Old Testament in Genesis 20 when Abraham prayed for healing, to the healing of nations in Revelations 22. Every prayer answered and every request granted at one extent. You must have faith. In Matthew 14:31 (NIV), "Immediately Jesus reached out his hand and caught him. "You of little faith," he said, "why did you doubt." Remember James 1:6-7 (NIV), "But when you ask, you must believe and not doubt, because the one who doubts is like a wave of the sea, blown and tossed by the wind. That person should not expect anything from the Lord." Honestly, I have faith that Jesus will heal me no matter what I've felt, no matter what I've said, no matter how many times I cursed His name out of ignorance or how many times I pushed Him away. Now I know…. His love flows from His heart to His healing hands. Mark 8:23 (AMP), "Taking the blind man by the hand, He brought him out of the village; and after spitting on his eyes and laying His hands on him, He asked him, "Do you see anything?" Mark

8:25 (AMP), "Then again He laid His hands on his eyes; and he looked intently and was restored and began to see everything clearly."

He will do the same for you if you have faith in Him. I do believe that sometimes God will move to heal someone with little faith, but we must remember, that our faith must be strong to maintain the healing. (Hebrews 11:1, Romans 10:17). I rely on both scriptures when my faith seems weak. With every scripture I set my heart to consume, I say them over and over until I'm engulfed in His presence and full of faith.

When I saw him, I fell at his feet as though dead. Then he placed his right hand on me and said: "Do not be afraid. I am the first and the last." Revelation 1:17 (GNT)

I have poured out my heart to you for almost four years. But only you who read this will know. I don't only want full revival for myself, I also want it for you. I've searched for almost thirty years to find out who I truly am. I would not have known the plans God had set for me if I hadn't relearned my authority and built up my faith in the word. My soul relies on faith to overcome past failures and storms. Failures disappear when I hear His word. My faith comes by hearing the word, reading the word, praying the word and singing the word.

I was listening to "So Will I" by Hillsong United yesterday and my heart sunk into the lyrics.

"And as You speak
A hundred billion failures disappear
Where you lost Your life so I could find it here
If you left the grave behind You so will I"

Finally, here it is, the answer to the biggest question about how to receive healing, and how to get over every heartache in your life, you must have faith; you must forgive; you must love; you must repent and change your ways to please God. We might slip up and sin but that's what Jesus died for; for us to be forgiven. It seems like a lot to ask to maintain our healing but when we fill ourselves with the word every day, we transform into warriors. It gives us purpose and strength to fight the good fight to resemble our Savior.

It has taken me so long to reach this state of confidence in the word. I am ashamed to admit it, but I believe it will be more beneficial to you to learn from my mistakes. I want to encourage you that no matter what your past looks like, you can become completely renewed by trusting in God. Trusting in his word that says whatever you ask for shall be yours, if its pleasing to God, …. Believe me He wants you Well, Healed and Restored.

Don't be afraid of the slight amount of doubt you have in your head. Just make sure there's no doubt in your heart. Pay more attention to the words that come out of your mouth. You claim Everything YOU SAY. …" There is power in the tongue". I am total proof of that. How many times do you get out of bed and claim a horrible day before it even starts? How many times have you lost hope in the power of God to change your circumstances? I raise my hand in truth. I am an example of this and look at the results. Do not follow in my foolish footsteps.

Claim the word and keep believing until you feel the power. Until you feel the comfort and love upon you. Don't give up! Again, James 1:6-7 (NIV)…" Do not doubt…. that person should not expect to receive anything from God". Faith is huge with God. If you start to feel an overwhelming fear or doubt, fix your eyes on the word. Think about the life of Abraham, the great man of faith. He never lost faith or hope that God would answer his prayers, and He did! Look at Romans 4:3 (NKJV), "Abraham believed God, and it was accounted to him for righteousness." And Job, wow. When his wife kept telling him "To give up the ghost and die" he never lost hope in the healing power of God.

Don't lose hope. The stronger you become in faith the more the devil will temp you and feed you lies. He will mislead you and misquote these scriptures. He will try to bring even more storms into yours and your family's lives. After reading this don't think "Then what's the use in living for God." We were given the power to move mountains with our mouths (See Mark 11:23 ESV). We have so much more power than most of us are aware of.

We have been taught our entire lives that the most powerful and most intelligent structure in our body is our mind. But in reality, the most powerful feature is our voice.

Chapter Eight
Forgiven

One of the biggest burdens in my life is not knowing who is to blame for my car wreck. Surely the devil was somehow responsible for this. (See 1 Peter 5:8 NIV). The police said I fell asleep, but I remember the lights and the music playing. My parents knew the man who hit me, and they know he was drunk because he lived close by and was drinking with his sister all night. So, was my life torn apart because I fell asleep or, was I hit by a drunk driver? I don't want to take the blame for this, but I can't imagine how someone could be innocent after stealing my belongings and leaving me there to die. This man dressed up as a nurse to spy on me. He stole scrubs from the ER, and he didn't even work at the hospital. He gave my parents some of my belongings and said the police told him to. He wasn't there because he was scared for me. He was there because he was scared for himself. His behavior led us to the truth, but I was never well enough to share it, until now. It wasn't until after I was released from Neuro-Trauma that my parents realized that their gas bill had tripled. My mom went to the gas station where the charges were coming from, and it happened to be that this man and his entire family used my gas card and signed my parent's names. Now tell me again, officer, that no one else was involved!

I know God wants me to forgive him. Matthew 6:14-15 (NIV), says, "For if you forgive other people when they sin against you, our heavenly Father will also forgive you. But if you do not forgive others their sins, your Father will not forgive your sins."

I could tell you that I forgave this man who stole everything from me. But there's an anger in my heart that I've held on to. I haven't allowed myself to let go. Why? After 3 decades I still haven't forgiven this man for the decisions he made that night. I suppose forgiving would have been easier if it hadn't affected my entire life.

I feel rage and resentment. Fury and wrath. This strong sense of hate is holding me captive. If I can't forgive this man, God can't forgive me! The evangelist, Mark, wrote in Mark 11:25 (ESV), "And whenever you stand praying, forgive, if you have anything against anyone, so that your Father also who is in heaven may forgive you your trespasses." Matthew 6:15 (ESV) confirms this, "But if you do not forgive others their trespasses, neither will your Father forgive your trespasses." (Luke 6:37 and Colossians 3:13 also claim this.) This heartache is wearing me down. I know I must forgive him. But how? I'm punishing myself with harboring frustration and ill will. To let go and move forward, I must remind myself that forgiving him doesn't mean he's not guilty. It just means I'm letting go of the pain he caused. Numbers 14:18 (ESV), reads, "The Lord is slow to anger and abounding in steadfast love, forgiving iniquity and transgression, but he will by no means clear the guilty." God will handle those who have wronged us, for He does not let the guilty go unpunished.

I found out that the man who hit me died a couple years ago. Now, I must forgive him. Numbers 15:28 (ESV), says "And the priest shall make atonement before the Lord for the person who makes a mistake, when he sins unintentionally, to make atonement for him, and he shall be forgiven." I've been so stuck in my own anguish I never even considered it until now. It's too late. I consider the fear he must have felt. Wondering what would happen to him if he stayed at the scene of the crime. Or maybe he didn't feel anything at all. If he had only known these scriptures. If only I had known these scriptures. Imagine our lives if we had.

What influenced me to be so angry and hateful toward my own family? Was it because I was depressed and drowning in sickness or was it because I was chained and broken by Satan? I guess I never considered the fear that flowed through their minds either as they made the decision to take my babies from me. All I could think of was the pain it caused me. Maybe I wasn't well enough to care for them all on my own….to tell you the truth, I wasn't. The amount of love I felt toward my boys was equal to the amount of suffering I felt after losing them. All this time I've thought of nothing other than how it affected me. I never really considered the struggles my family faced. I only considered my own. I understand now that my parents didn't take my babies out of selfishness. Though it stole ten years of my life, my parents gave my boys a life I was incapable of giving them. If they hadn't been there to help me care for my babies, I would have lost them completely….and in reality, that would have been much worse. I've sorted it out in my mind and confirmed it in my heart. Their actions weren't meant to hurt me. They were meant to protect us all.

I really loved my endocrinologist, Dr. Maruca. I saw him so much he became family. I always admired his intelligence while he watched me constantly struggle with mine. For so long, all I wanted was his acceptance. For him to see me as more than a sick patient. To see me as more than defeated. He saved my life in the beginning, but I feel like he gave up on me in the end. I was angry but I'm not anymore. I'm filling my heart with joyful memories. Like the first time he gave me a job so he could watch my development…and when he hired me back after I threw a tantrum and quit. I cried for so many years, unaware that he accepted me the first day he saved my life. He meant so much to me, I couldn't bear the thought of him loving another patient more than me. I know he did all he knew how to do. I had too much faith in a doctor to perform miracles that only God has the power to perform.

Colossians 3:13 (NIV), advises us to… "Bear with each other and forgive one another if any of you has a grievance against someone. Forgive as the Lord forgave you".

Figuring this out has cleansed years of anger and pain. I didn't do this on my own and I've known it from the first day God told me to write my testimony. I understand I have a purpose, but I can't fulfill it until I forgive. The years I've lost in my life are a tragedy. Every dark night and lonely day. Ignorant of the word and running out of people to blame. If only I had recognized the corporate in the mirror.

Now I see myself. I see my faults and I know how to overcome them. I have no one to blame for my life but myself. I was given a choice the day I learned who God was. I had a choice to learn more about Him or go on with my life. I chose the wrong direction. I paid the price. But now, because of the word, my path has been straightened. (See Proverbs 3:6 ESV). The light of God is shown in every verse and every page that fills my heart, mind and soul. Every word that says I have authority, and every scripture that says I am forgiven.

We "have authority to cast out demons" (Mark 3:15 ESV), and the love and power from God to forgive as the Lord forgave us, (See Colossians 3:14 ESV).

I know, the more you think about it, the angrier you become. It builds up and you're left with yet another choice. You either swallow your words or let the power of your words ruin your life, like I did. I was drowning in the un-forgiveness that fueled my anger. The anger outweighed forgiveness and I was lost in the world. I bled in the memory of painful scars.

To the mental trauma caused by innocent betrayal, I rebuke you and chose to forgive. My heart has been cleansed and I find victory in letting go. Every person involved in my life, through the good and the bad, have become a part of me. You've led me to this day, and I no longer consider the loss. I forgive you.

Ephesians 4:32 (ESV), "Be kind to one another, tenderhearted, forgiving one another, as God in Christ forgave you."

Chapter Nine
A Minute in Paradise

Incase you were wondering, I had already planned to tell you about my travel to the Heavens…and hell. But first, I'm going to ask you to be open-minded and willing to accept that anything is possible.

Genesis 1:1 (KJV) says, "In the beginning, God created the HEAVEN**S.**" If you study the scriptures, you will read that there are three heavens. The fact that Jesus passed through the heavens gives evidence there is more than one heaven. (See Hebrew 4:14 KJV). From what I have learned, the first of the heavens, the atmospheric heavens, is earth itself. It includes the air we breathe and the space that surrounds us. Deuteronomy 11:17 (KJV) says, "And then the Lord's wrath be kindled against you, and he shut up the heaven, that there be no rain, and that the land yield not her fruit." Three more scriptures confirm this heaven in Deuteronomy 28:12, Judges 5:4, and Acts 14:17. The second of the heavens, the celestial heavens, is outer space. In Psalm 19:4-6 (BSB), we learn that "…. In the heavens, he has pitched a tent for the sun. Its rising is from one end of the heavens and its circuit to the other end." There are more scriptures to support this; Deuteronomy 17:3, Jeremiah 8:2 and Isaiah 13:10. In 2 Corinthians 12:2 (KJV), Apostle Paul said…" I knew a man in Christ above fourteen years ago (whether in the body, I cannot tell; or whether out of the body, I cannot tell: God knows) such a one caught up to the third heaven." The third heaven is the heaven of heavens, the Throne of God, the highest heaven, paradise. (See Deuteronomy 10:14, 1 Kings 8:30, Psalms 2:4, Matthew 5:16, Deuteronomy 10:14, 1 King 8:27, and 2 Chronicles 2:6.)

I never entered this third heaven. I was stranded in the second of three heavens, the celestial heavens. It was there that I envisioned the gates of the third heavens… but I never walked through them.

Though decades apart, it felt like I was right below the heaven of heavens. I absorbed the comforting peace and heard the angels singing. A power immediately covered me with internal warmth while my external body froze. My faith was weak, and I was full of fear. Chills ran down my spine…According to Kenneth E. Hagan, the celestial heavens are where spirits live. That must be why I could feel the evil pass through my flesh.

I felt an overpowering force pulling me further and further down while a stronger sense of love held me in place. It felt as if I was chained to hell, but I wasn't strong enough to escape. The further I fell, the weaker I became. The more I gave up, the faster I fell. I finally fought back and called His name. The name above all names is Jesus. I gave Him my heart, and He broke my chains.

The Mercy of God suspended me in the air while I was lifted higher and higher toward the light. I could see the emeralds and diamonds shining in front of the entrance to victory. The higher I rose, the faster I flew. I crossed the celestial barrier and arrived in the heavenly. Chills faded, and comfort was laid upon me like a warm blanket. I escaped through the clouds and ran up the stairs.

Beauty stood before me, and I wept with joy. I was close enough to touch the rubies and open the golden gates. But they were unreachable. I cried for my Shepard, Jesus, and he met me in space. The gates were closed to me, and I fell back to earth. As soon as my soul reunited with my body, I awoke.

For almost 30 years, no one has believed that I experienced this. It was beyond their understanding. It was beyond my understanding, but I've never felt anything more real. The colors were beyond imaginable. The sense of well-being and confidence was as vibrant as the light shining from God. All these years I was unable to explain my experience. The Holy Spirit has guided me through this book to explain what others would see as a dream. As many would define it, a fantasy.

The same children of God who deny testimonies of heaven yet fear the end of the world.

Numerous people have told me that they've been hearing for years that the end of the world was near. Well, I am sure you would agree that signs and wonders prove we are living in the last days. But the last days of what? Is this really the end...or just a glimpse of what's to come? While cuffed to his cell, Paul warns us in 2 Timothy 3:1-17 (ESV), "But understand this that in the last days, there will come times of difficulty. For people will be lovers of self, lovers of money, proud, arrogant, abusive, disobedient to their parents, ungrateful, unholy, heartless, unappeasable, slanderous, without self-control, brutal, not loving good, treacherous, reckless, swollen with conceit, lovers of pleasure rather than lovers of God, having the appearance of godliness, but denying it's power…"

In 2021, the fear of a communist nation took ground over the United States as Satan's realm stole our Presidential election. As the majority of Christians considered the signs and wonders as end times. The confusion startled me, and I was curious as to where God was in the middle of this tragedy. I was encouraged by my friend, Rene, to listen to the prophets on Elijah List. I was immediately hooked. Kat Kerr, Robin Bullock, and Johnny Enlow opened a new door in my life to the prophetic. I've taken spiritual warfare classes, and their knowledge truly lines up with the Word of God. It was comforting to hear Kat Kerr say in January of 2021, "Calm down, calm down, this had to take place to expose the evil." The timelines and prophecies have all lined up in order of what each of these prophets has prophesied. They assured us that God would protect the righteous through these horrific trials, and He has. (See John 16:33).

Today, I heard Johnny Enlow, an end-time prophet, talk about the three Heavens, and I was encouraged by the Holy Spirit to share his explanation. This prophetic description aligns with mine, and here is what God wants us to know about why our prayers may not have been answered.

Keep in mind these statements are not word for word but a summary of Johnny Enlow's description of the three Heavens. Remember, we are talking in an area of mystery.

"... Listen and follow [carefully] the words of my servants, the prophets whom I have been sending to you time and time again, though you did not listen."

Jeremiah 26:5, Amplified Bible

"The first heavens is what we're exposed to, the realm of light, our heaven. The second heavens is a realm to which the demonic realm has been confined. If they weren't confined there, we would be facing too big of a battle if we saw the number and size of what's against us. Their access to our realm is given to them through influence and authority given to them by our own sins. The third realm is Heaven's realm. Demons do not have access to the throne room, the Holy City. The whole spirit realm is under the third heaven. Creatures from the 3rd heaven have access to the 1st and 2nd heavens. There are people who know how to access those heavens. It's the dark realm where you can see the planning of the enemy, what he's planning on doing to a person or a nation. Elijah, a prophet of God (See 1 Kings 18-22), had the capability of listening in on the enemy on that level but was usually attacked more because of that. The enemy's plan was always to kill, steal, and destroy. If the enemy is planning a plot against you, go higher."

The first heaven is our realm, the third Heaven is God's realm, and the second Heaven is the interference realm. Johnny Enlow said that many prophets have said that any prayer that makes it to the third heavens is answered. Suppose you get through the interference realm. That's the resistance realm between us and the throne room. Satan is a legalist. He has a massive contingency. He has his own legal firm. When prayers come up, the demons bring accusations against the person asking, from some level of sin. They block the prayer for legal matters. You can cause combat in the courts of heaven by saying, I guess God didn't hear my prayer". The demons will say these people don't really have faith; by law, you can't answer their prayers. Second heaven interference is mostly over legal matters. Because of sin and interference, God may not have heard your prayers. There are scriptures that say you asked, but I didn't hear your prayer. (See Jeremiah 11:14). There are prayers that don't even make it to a hearing to the Father because they legally get blocked. Lucifer's name is "accuser". You could be praying and fasting, and the accuser can say, "You can't answer their prayer; they haven't forgiven so and so." If we have unforgiveness, it will somehow affect our prayer life. This legalist army will interfere and block our prayers from being answered. So, here's the mystery: forgive so your prayers will be answered.

Are you bringing hope to people? Then, the enemy wants to kill you. Go above and seek the Lord's coverage. He sits in Heaven and laughs at the enemy's plans, so we should too." (End quote.)

"But the One who rules in heaven laughs. The Lord scoffs at them."

Psalm 2:4 (NLT)

Interesting…but what about tongues? What we pray in tongues bypasses the celestial heavens because neither satan nor his disgusting demons can interpret it. Whether the devil could hear my prayers or not, I have the power to tell him to let go of my blessings. I learned that in Kenneth E Hagin's book, Faith Takes Back What The Devil Stole.

So, Heaven is a real place, and it's more amazing than words can illustrate. It was the first and last time I've ever felt peace and wholeness. But hell, that's another story. It's so horrible, I don't even want to explain it, but I feel led to. The three minutes I disappeared from this earth played hours in the abyss. I was unaware of how to expound such an experience in the presence of complete darkness. After reading about Kenneth E. Hagin's trip to hell, I realized I wasn't dreaming when my skin turned to flames. My story is similar to Pastor Hagin's description of Hades in his book, I Went To Hell…

Chapter 1, The Church Member Who Went to Hell…

"I began to descend down, down, into a pit, like you'd go down into a well, cavern, or cave. I did not know that my physical voice picked that up. As I was trying to say goodbye, I knew I was going down into that place. All three of my family members who were present testified later, 'When you said good-bye, your voice sounded like you were way down in a cave or cavern or something.'

And I continued to descend. I went down feet first, down, down, down, down. I could look up and see the lights on earth. They finally faded away. Darkness encompassed me 'round about, darkness that is blacker than any night man has ever seen. It seemed that if you had a knife, you could cut a chunk of it out. You couldn't see your hand if it was one inch in front of your nose.

The farther down I went, the darker it became, and the hotter it became, until finally, way down beneath me, I could see fingers of light playing on the wall of darkness. And I came to the bottom of the pit.

...

I was pulled toward hell just like a magnet draws metal unto itself. I knew that once I entered through those gates, I could not come back. I endeavored to slow my descent, because when I came to the bottom of the pit, there still was a slant downward.

I was conscious of the fact that some kind of creature met me at the bottom of that pit. I didn't look at it. My gaze was riveted on the gates, yet I knew that a creature was there by my right side..." Kenneth E Hagin

Chapter 3, Dying without God...

"I took her hand, and she said, 'Oh, Kenneth, Kenneth! You're a preacher; tell me there is no hell! Oh, tell me! I said there wasn't any hell. I said there wasn't any. I said every preacher ought to be killed. I'm afraid! I'm afraid! It's so dark, It's so dark. IT'S SO DARK. IT'S SO DARK. It's ...,' And she fell back on the pillow. We couldn't get through to her. And she died and went to hell, crying, 'It's so dark! It's so dark'..."
Kenneth E. Hagin

I remember that darkness. I was embodied by it as soon as I closed my eyes. Drugged with sleeping pills and bleeding excessively from the ccsarian, I remember the doctors constantly telling me, "Don't close your eyes"! "Don't close your eyes"! As the nurses showed me Baby C, my body and spirit idled at peace, knowing the suffering was almost over. I closed my eyes, believing my boys would live and I could "rest in peace." But that's not what happened. I hadn't repented. I hadn't accepted Christ into my life again. I wasn't protected by the blood of Jesus. No. I was bleeding from the fire that tore my carnal mind as I fell further and further into hell. The further I fell, the hotter it became. The sun disappeared as it swallowed the air. Falling further and further and gasping and gasping to breathe. Immense physical pain and mental torture encompassed my whole existence. The Spirit of God was absent from the atmosphere. The spirit of love, compassion, comfort, and joy was obsolete. Without God there was only sorrow and pain. Cries from inmates echoed throughout the dungeon as maggots ate their flesh. The only lights that shined in hell were the flames that pierced every soul. Screams of terror came from every prison wall, where each prisoner awaited their torture in isolation. Alone in darkness and separated from God.

…"The snares of death encompassed me; the pangs of Sheol (hell, a place of darkness) laid hold on me; I suffered distress and anguish.
Psalm 116:3 (ESV).

Jesus recounted hell as nothingness, a place that has no life or light in it. (See Matthew 10:28).

It was by the grace of God that I called for the name of His son. As I fell to the bottom of the pit, demons took hold of me and dragged me towards the gates of hell. I cried out His Name, "Jesus." (If only I had known sooner that the password to get out of hell was the Name Above All Names.) I remember the fear in their disgusting, monstrous, monkey faces as they were forced by the power of His name to release me. I was no longer held captive by the absence of light; I was in the arms of my Savior. I escaped hell and, in a second, awoke from darkness.

Mark 16:17 (NIV), "And these signs will accompany those who believe; IN MY NAME they will drive out demons..."

I burned from the fires of hell and healed in the light of God. I fear for any of you who do not believe Satan is real. Though I understand how you could be misled. My husband and I were, unfortunately, very influenced by a man that pushed the idea into our brains that Satan was fictional. I believed this for well over ten years and severely suffered the consequences. I am fully aware now that Satan exists. The years I denied his existence only gave him more power over my life. For over 20 years, I relied on doctors when I should have relied on God.

The Bible teaches in multiple scriptures that people die from lack of knowledge. In the book of Job 36:12 (NIV), he writes, "But if they do not listen, they will perish by the sword and die without knowledge." (It is believed that Solomon wrote most of Proverbs.) In Proverbs 5:23 (NIV), he explains, "For lack of discipline they will die, led astray by their own great folly." In Proverbs 10:21 (NIV), his statement is rephrased, "The lips of the righteous nourish many, but fools die from lack of sense.

I suffered the effects of living without God until I learned that He is my everything, my all in all. (Colossians 1:17 KJV). You need to understand what you're truly getting yourself into when you reject Christ as your Savior. As soon as I gave up my power over Satan, he took complete possession of me. I was left full of weakness, sorrow, and fear. Out of ignorance, I lost everything. But through faith in the Word of God, I've been rescued from hell.

It has taken almost 30 years for me to accept the traumas I've faced in my life. I've found peace in the Word of God because His mercy has shown me that in this world, we all struggle to hold on to hope. But we don't have to struggle when we understand our authority over the devil.

"Listen carefully: I have given you authority (that you now possess) to tread on serpents and scorpions, and (the ability to exercise authority over all the power of the enemy (Satan); and nothing will (in any way) harm you."
Luke 10:19 (AMP)

Breaking the chain of storms in your life depends on how you use your authority. "Submit yourselves therefore to God. Resist the devil, and he will flee from you." James 4:7 (KJV)

"Finally, be strong in the Lord and in his mighty power. Put on the full armor of God so that you can take your stand against the devil's schemes. For our struggle is not against flesh and blood but against the rulers, against the authorities, against the peers of the dark world, and against the spiritual forces. When the day of evil comes, you may be able to stand your ground after you have done everything to stand. Stand firm, then, with the belt of truth buckled around your waist, with the breastplate of righteousness in place, and with your feet fitted with the readiness that comes from the gospel of peace. In addition to all this, take up the shield of faith, with which you can extinguish all the flaming arrows of the evil

one. Take the helmet of salvation and sword of the Spirit, which is the word of God."
Ephesians 6:10-18 (NIV)

In my lifetime, I've torn through the shackles of affliction. I've escaped through the Heavens. I've circled the end of the earth. I've felt the power in my armor and burned through the gates of hell.

"Enter through the narrow gate; for the gate is wide and the way is broad that leads to destruction, and there are many who enter through it. For the gate is small and the way is narrow that leads to life, and there are few who find it."
Matthew 7:13-14 (NASB)

Chapter Ten
Saved by Grace

I dedicate this chapter to my best friend, my cat, LuLu.

July 5, 2005 to January 30, 2024

For 12 years my closest companion has been my cat. I adore her. I've always loved cats, and I don't know how I would be able to live without mine. She had always been my comforter before I found Christ. She hid with me in fear and fought with me through the darkness. I lay in terror each night, but she was never afraid. As soon as the light was absent, darkness appeared. It appeared in many forms, but she stayed by my side through it all. She witnessed every nail that penetrated my flesh and every beast that tormented my mind. She never ran. She fought to shield me and heal my deepest wounds. She would sleep right next to me or sometimes right on top of me. She would purr to soothe the aches and pains from years of being chained to a bed. She was my company when I was lonely and love when I felt none. She filled the hole in my heart and gave me a reason to wake up every day. I've loved her since the first time I held her when she was a sick little kitten. I nursed her back to life and with the help of God, she restored mine.

Right before becoming severely ill in 2005, I experienced the fear of losing her. I remember when we were getting hardwood flooring in the house, and she swallowed a piece of cork. (At the time, I was not aware of that.) She wouldn't stop throwing up. I was bawling with stress as I rushed her to the vet. They took multiple X-rays and couldn't find anything. So, the vet's only choice was exploratory surgery. I was not allowed to stay and wait through the surgery. The veterinarian made me go home. I remember lying in bed crying for hours. I couldn't bear the thought of losing her. She was the only one who understood my mental and physical inflictions. I prayed but had no faith. I cried all day until the veterinarian contacted me to say that LuLu had recovered. I paced and wept all night until I could pick her up the next morning. Back then, I didn't even know what faith was, but somehow, my prayers were answered. His love resurrected me that day.

I prayed for LuLu, and by faith, I thanked God for healing her. I lay hands on her and claim health over her body and mind. I love her, and I know she loves me. I can't imagine my life without her. But I do know that no matter who ascends first, we will be together for eternity. She was a gift from God. Even when I had no faith, God knew what lay ahead and had mercy on me. He saved her life. He saved her life for me. And she saved mine.

"The eyes of all creatures look to you, and you give them their food at the proper time. You open your hand, and you satisfy the desire of every living thing. The Lord is fair in all his ways and faithful in everything he does." Psalm 145:15-17 (GWT)

It was never a concern to me that I tend to care more about the well-being of animals than people. Maybe it's because I have never been made fun of by my cat. She doesn't tell me I'm stupid or use me for her own amusement…like my "friends" in high school did. That doesn't mean I don't love people. I guess I just don't trust most of them because they've let me down so many times.

I took a test a couple of years ago to find out what my redemptive gifts are. After completing it, I learned that my gifts are a prophet, giver, and mercy. God made me to be this person to use my gifts to help others. I want you to know that we all have redemptive gifts, and according to Paul in Romans 12:6-8 (ESV), we're supposed to use them…"Having gifts that differ according to the grace given to us, let us use them: if prophecy, proportion to our faith; if service, in our serving; the one who teaches, in his teaching; the one who exhorts, in his exhortation; the one who contributes, in generosity; the one who leads, with zeal; the one who does acts of mercy, with cheerfulness."

Do you ever wonder why God even created you? I did for over 20 years. As soon as I found out my purpose in life, my desire to live became stronger. I have a foundation set before me. I have a path to follow. But the adversary does not want me to succeed. So, for the past month, I've been struggling to finish these chapters. The fatigue and stress are overwhelming as my desire to achieve grows stronger. Though every force of evil is against me, a stronger force of love is always there to give me strength to continue. I'm here. I'm typing, and LuLu is right beside me. I refuse to fall short of His glory, for every battle gives light to His presence and faith that He has already absolved our trials.

His love has saved me, and by Grace, His love saved LuLu. When I was unaware of the truth and full of sin, He held out His hand and saved me. I finally gave my heart and soul to Christ, and now I am redeemed.

The dictionary defines redemption as:

1. The action of saving or being saved from sin, error, or evil.
2. The action of regaining or gaining possession of something in exchange for payment or clearing a debt.

Romans 5:8-11 (AMP) specifies, "God clearly shows and proves His own love for us, by the fact that while we were still sinners, Christ died for us. Therefore, since we have now been justified [declared free of the guilt of sin] by His blood, [how much more certain is it that we will be saved from the wrath of God through Him? For while we were enemies, we were reconciled to God through the death of His Son. It is much more certain, having been reconciled, that we will be saved [from the consequences of sin] by His life [that is, we will be saved because Christ lives today]."

We have already been redeemed through the blood of Christ, and our redemption is necessary to fulfill His promise.

Ephesians 1:7 (ESV) explains, "In Him we have redemption through his blood, the forgiveness of our trespasses, according to the riches of His graces…"

I am redeemed, I am forgiven, and my debt was paid in full the day my savior died for me. Though I wouldn't know any of this if I hadn't gone back to a faith-based, spirit-filled church. I wouldn't have known how to maintain faith to keep my little companion full of life. I remember attending church three days a week and I was still unaware of my authority and still very ill. I really didn't learn how to achieve the desires of my heart until I began to study on my own. I still attend church regularly because my spirit filled church is prepared to restore me. The Holy Spirit surrounds me and by the end of the service I am filled with hope and strength to face each day. I have hope that my little LuLu will have a long and healthy life and that I have the power to claim and stand on that. I learned this at a true faith-based church. Constantly full of the spirit, the Holy Spirit. It's the Holy Spirit that fills you with joy and laughter...and courage. Courage to share your testimony with the world in hope to save others. Courage to keep standing in faith that your animals are healed.

After graduation from Rhema Bible College, I realized that I had read more books than I thought was humanly possible...and I am so grateful. What I have learned more than anything by attending Rhema, is exactly what my heart desired, faith. Faith in believing that whatever I say shall be. Faith in the word that says God wants me well and that he wants our pets well. Most of all, the power of my own words can either enlighten me or break me. The words I speak over LuLu can be life or death.

I've spent the last three years speaking life over my best friend. Praying Psalm 91 day and night for God to restore her life. When she was about to turn 10 years old, in human years, I felt a spirit of fear over me. Fear of losing her. That fear stole every day of my life. I cried at just the thought of losing LuLu. I cried every day, dreading that day. So, I did everything I possibly could to prolong her life. To tell you the truth, I think I did too much, and maybe that's why she got so sick.

Two years of constant gastrointestinal distress. Did I give her too many supplements? Did I take her to her vet too often? She became so sick that I had to give her a bath two or more times a day. At the end of every dreadful day, I would fall on the ground broken and lost as I watched her suffer.

It's like God allowed me to fall apart. He was waiting for me to catch an epiphany, to open my eyes and ears. But I was so broken I couldn't see the signs, let alone hear them. I finally opened my mouth to speak to God. I spoke to Him in an unknown language. It was then that I heard the Holy Spirit say, "What are you doing? Use your authority!"

I jumped up and started commanding healing over LuLu. I called down hosts and angels to fight the attacks against us and cast out darkness. I stood on the word and every prayer I made. I stood on the promises of Christ, our Savior. In faith, I praised God through this horrible storm, all day and all night…and it worked…for two years.

The fear that tried to encapsulate me, drowning me with constant fear and sorrow, wondering how much time I had left with her, but the time just kept pushing me toward that tragic day. The day I dreaded for almost 20 years.

I rushed LuLu to an emergency veterinarian around midnight on the morning of January 29th, 2024. The vet insisted it was time to let her go. As she rambled on, I cursed every word that came out of her mouth. I thought, if God directed me on how to save her life last time, he will do it again. But deep down inside I could feel Jesus holding me tightly, preparing me for what was to come. The next morning, I drove LuLu to her veterinarian. I had to leave her there for the doctor to examine her throughout the day. As I drove off, I cried wondering if I would ever get to take her home again. I imagined holding her in my arms and kissing her forehead, like I do every day.

After hours of pleading with God to prolong LuLu's life, I received the call. My heart dropped when I answered. Knowing I'm not supposed to fear anything but at the same time I was afraid. But it was good news, or so I thought. All our veterinarian said was "We did it last time. We can do it again." So, I was advised to medicate her with an emergency medication every two hours. I was on board. "Yes, that's it," I told myself. "He will do it again" … but deep down inside the comforter was holding on tighter than usual. It was 2200 and time for another dose. I fought to keep a mindset of expectancy but at the same time I felt hesitant. I gave her the syringe and kissed her on the nose. I claimed Psalm 91 prayer over her with pure frankincense oil that my friend Brandy prayed over. I lay next to her on my bed and watched her sister, Lolly, cuddle her tightly as if she knew this was their last time together. I prayed and cried and rebuked and commanded. I did everything I knew how to do in my God given power. But when midnight hit and it was time for another dose of medicine, I heard the Lord say, "No more." I wept with fear and great sorrow. I hadn't slept for 3 straight days. I felt like I was floating. I thought maybe this is just a nightmare and it was, but I was wide awake.

Around 0200 I heard LuLu gasp and fall over on the floor. My son, Gavin, lifted her up in his arms and carried her to my bed. I laid her on top of her favorite blanket. I sat next to LuLu and cried "Jesus I give up! Take her! She's yours!" And in a flash, she was gone. I've never had a prayer answered so quickly.

I sat there in a state of disbelief, confusion and exhaustion. I was so tired I thought I was hallucinating when I saw two lights appear right above LuLu's body. About 6 inches from my face stood a white light and a black light floating in the air. These lights were alive. The white light was in front as the black light lagged, behind. I stared into the white light as if in a daze. As the lights floated in the air, they remained motionless. It felt like eternity as I waited to see what would happen next. Suddenly, the black light fell on the ground and depleted. It dissolved like a particle in the air. It completely disappeared. My focus remained on the white light as it seemed to keep its focus on me. I said "I love you LuLu. You're free." At that second the white light shot right through my heart and flew up through the roof.

Staggered by everything I had just witnessed, I messaged my friend, Carolyn, who I consider my great spiritual counselor. She told me the black light was the suffering she left behind and the white light was her freedom. She pierced through my flesh to leave a mark in my heart. A mark of love that will remain a treasure until the day I get to kiss her forehead and hold her in my arms again.

Psalms 91 Prayer (Psalm 91:1-16)

Whoever dwells in the shelter of the Most High

will rest in the shadow of the Almighty.

I will say of the Lord, "He is my refuge and my

Fortress,

My God, in whom I trust."

Surely, he will save you from the fowler's snare

And from the deadly pestilence.

He will cover you with his feathers,

And under his wings you will find refuge;

His faithfulness will be your shield and rampart,

You will not fear the terror of night

Nor the arrow that flies by day

108

Nor the pestilence that stalks in the darkness,

Not the plaque that destroys at midday.

A thousand may fall at your side,

Ten thousand at your right hand,

But it will not come near you

You will only observe with your eyes

And see the punishment of the wicked.

If you say, "The Lord is my refuge,"

and you make the Most High your dwelling,

no harm will overtake you,

no disaster will come near your tent.

For he will command his angels concerning you

To guard you in all your ways;

They will lift you up in their hands,

For so that you will not strike your foot

Against a stone.

You will tread on the lion and the cobra;

You will trample the great lion and the serpent.

"Because he loves me," says the Lord, "I will rescue him;

I will protect him, for he acknowledges my name.

He will call on me, and I will answer him;

I will be with him in trouble,

I will deliver him and honor him.

With long life I will satisfy him

And show him my salvation."

Chapter Eleven
Good Bye Mary Jane

I use Cannabis as a replacement for synthetic medications. So, before you read this chapter, I ask that you open your heart and mind. There are many things we, as humans, refuse to agree on. I hope that you will read this entire chapter and the rest of my testimony because I don't want you to miss the victory in the end. I want you to understand that I would not have lived to share my story without medical cannabis. Keep in mind I Peter 5:8 (ESV) that tells us to "Be sober-minded; be watchful…". You can use cannabis and still obey God's word. You don't have to get high. If you do, I won't judge you. That's honestly the state I was in for the last three years. But I was healing.

Shortly after I awoke from the coma in 1993, everyone started giving me cannabis. Even my neurologist wasn't against the idea. I thought it was so odd that everyone was giving me this so called "medicine." I had just been told before the car wreck that only "losers" used it. I didn't know how to think on my own, so I took the medicine….and I'm glad I did. Somehow, I relearned everything faster and amazed my doctors with a much quicker recovery. They had assumed that after two massive head injuries, I'd spend the rest of my life staring at a wall. But I surpassed their expectations and graduated with my class. I was doing so well…. but then, all the sudden, everyone stopped giving me the medicine that decreased the seizures and helped me sleep. All they gave me were lies about the side effects. Out of ignorance, I believed them. I wouldn't have suffered for so long if I had just followed my instinct. But I didn't. I followed everyone else's. I listened to their unscriptural opinions and suffered through their judgments. Even though I wasn't doing anything wrong. They judged me even though they had no idea what it was like to be me. I stopped taking the medicine that was making me well and gave up on the One who already did. I slowly became weaker and weaker, and I eventually gave up on God. I lay in bed suffering, depleting and no longer thriving. I didn't have the energy to open the Bible, and I had no one to preach to me. Finally, ten years later, my mom looked past everyone else's opinion and investigated the facts herself. She took me to my first medical dispensary in De Beque, Co where I was treated with CBD.

According to Cannabis Clinicians Colorado, the most important thing for us to know is that you can't die from using oil or flour. I have heard you can overdose on edibles though. According to these specialists, Cannabis can treat Cancer, Severe Pain, In Lieu of an Opiate, Seizures including Epilepsy, Glaucoma, Persistent Muscle Spasms, including Multiple Sclerosis, HIV/AIDS, Server Nausea, Cachexia, Physical Wasting, Autism Spectrum Disorder and PTSD, (Post Traumatic Stress Disorder). This medicine has no side effects, no long term negative effects.... actually, no negative effects at all, unless you overuse it. I can honestly say, the number of seizures I have a year has greatly reduced. I used to have seizures 2-10 times a day. Now I only have them 2-10 times a year. But I'm believing I will soon have none because I trust the scriptures that say so.

I suggest looking up these facts to better determine your feelings toward this miraculous plant.

When I first started taking cannabis, I took it in the oil form, but it wasn't strong enough. I still couldn't get out of bed. My fatigue was unimaginable. A doctor suggested that I try cannabis in flower to increase my serotonin and in turn produce energy. At first, I took it in moderation but quickly began to rely on it too much. I was relying on the power of a plant over the power of God to heal me. I only used Medical Cannabis for a couple of years until I realized I was depending on it way too much. Proverbs 3:5 (ESV) advises us to "Trust in the Lord with all your heart, and do not lean on your own understanding." I would wake up every day weak and angry and my only relief was CBD or cannabis. I fought to claim

His name every day and with doubt I never waited on the Lord to answer my prayers. Isaiah 40:31 (ESV) explains, "But they who wait for the Lord shall renew their strength; they shall mount up with wings like eagles; they shall run and not be weary; they shall walk and not faint."

The fact that Medical Cannabis became legal in Colorado has angered so many people because they refuse to learn the truth for themselves. I was desperate and dying and had no way out. My doctors gave up on me and stopped trying to save my life. Cannabis was the only way I made it to church. But as soon as I stepped out in faith, God carried me the rest of the way. Finally, after struggling for so many years, everything in my life is finally weighing out. When the knowledge in scriptures fills my mind and soul, I can ask God anything and trust my Guardian angel to follow His command. "You have been given the authority of Jesus Christ, as an heir, and you can command your angels to move on your behalf to carry out the Word." Psalm 103:20 (ESV).

I find no reason in judging someone for choosing a natural source over prescription medication. In a sense, everything God made on this earth was made to heal us, nutritionally, emotionally and physically. After years of swallowing synthetic medications and applying chemicals to my body, I have chosen to only use organic ingredients and honestly, I feel so much healthier. It's amazing how many lessons I have learned from all the mistakes I've made in my life. But these mistakes have sculpted me into who I am today, and the lessons have taught me how to not make them again.

After writing this chapter and after reading this testimony we should all have greater faith in the word even though we all lead different paths in life. I drove on a windy road for most of my life, but by faith in God, I am steady on a straight path and I'm no longer car sick. (Proverbs 3:6 KJV). I am no longer on the path to recovery. I'm already healed.

"…He was wounded for our transgressions, He was bruised for our iniquities; The chastisement for our peace was upon Him, And by His stripes we are healed." Isaiah 53:5 (NKJV)

If you don't already know the magic of marijuana, imagine 24 hours of weakness, depression and failure. It was amazing the first time I tried it. I instantly had energy to get out of bed, regularly attend a faith-based church and a Christian Bible College. I have faith now because I constantly surrendered to the word of God. I'm well and finally, after twelve years, I have my boys back. For over 20 years I thought this was the end. I assumed I would never accomplish any of my dreams in life. For me, the side effects of Cannabis are health, and this new health has turned my ignorance into faith. The strength of God and years of using cannabis as a replacement for serotonin, dopamine and melatonin, has filled me with the desire to succeed. After 27 years of struggling to make it through each day, I finally beat the curse. I have accomplished more than I ever thought was possible.

One day, while in the presence of His love, I envisioned Philippians 4:13 (KJV). From that day forward, I continue to claim, "I can do all things through Christ who strengthens me." Jesus taught me how to have strength when I had no faith. He taught me how to dose and how to let go. He showed me that all I ever needed was Him.

I will admit that I still use cannabis for minor aches and pains, illness or difficult days. But it is not my most reliable source. I will never stop claiming I am "Healed by His stripes" (Isaiah 53:5 NKJV) and I will never rely on the strength of this natural medicine over the strength God has already blessed me with. I am sharing this with you because I don't want you to be ashamed if you rely on Cannabis. When I did, twenty-four hours a day, it became more of a burden. I realized I was overusing it to stay awake, to sleep and to block every pain in my life. Consequently, every time I felt depressed, anxious or stressed, I took more and every fear in my life would disappear…. even though the answers were there all along. I understood the scriptures that encourage me to rely on Christ over anyone or anything. I know my authority. (See Jeremiah 29:11 ESV).

I want you to understand that there is a way to get out of bed every morning. There is a way to live without constant pain. There is way to feel well enough to open your bible and learn your authority over sickness and disease.

I will admit that I have experienced a horrible panic attack before. I crawled under my covers and hid in fear. It was horrible. But then I remembered what Pastor John said about our authority over medications. We have the authority to claim whatever we say shall be. We have the authority to tell our medications to only replace and repair. We have the authority to tell the side effects to leave….and go back to hell…. because God did not give us a spirit of fear. "For God has not given us a spirt of fear, but of power and of love and of a sound mind". Timothy 1:7 (NKJV).

 I have authority to tell the side effects of my prescription medications not to touch me. But the side effects of Cannabis are the reason why I use it. It's a pain reliever, without the side effects of aspirin and ibuprofen. It's an antidepressant without jitters and a sleeping pill without drowsiness. This medicine wasn't man made. It was God made. The only natural medicine I know of that replicate and imitate the function of neurotransmitters. As sativa gives a boost of serotonin, indica acts as a replica of dopamine and melatonin.

I thank God for helping me write this chapter. I almost didn't because I was uncertain as to how it might interfere with the way you view my testimony. I don't want you to feel this way because for months I have mainly struggled to finish this book, for you.

I asked myself, what better way is there to bring people to God and share these scriptures that prove healing? What better way is there to teach as many people as I can possibly reach to tell them the truth about this miraculous medicine. This natural plant has helped me heal physically and mentally. It demolished every symptom of pain in my body. Its healing ingredients gave me great energy and a great want to succeed. I believe it was planted by God to heal us. I relied on its flower and oils to help me function and sleep for well over three years and it changed me.

It has changed who I am. It has changed the way I view life. It has changed everything about me, even my faith. I do believe God led me to this seed-bearing herb and a future that I was unable to achieve on my own. Most of all, cannabis gave me the physical ability to reach out to God and allow Him to fulfill my purpose.

I know the plans he has for me; to give me hope and a future. (See Jeremiah 29:11 NIV). Now I know, by faith, I have to say goodbye Mary Jane. I have to say goodbye to constant dependence. To the fear of not having this medicine in my hands 24 hours a day. But I have no reason, or plan, in discontinuing my use of this miraculous plant. It's my daily vitamin that takes better care of me than any prescription could provide. I have relied on Cannabis for a total of 7 years. For now, I believe it will always be available in my home, but I will no longer reach for a plant to heal me. I will raise my hands to my Great Physician.

…They that are whole have no need of the physician, but they that are sick: I came not to call the righteous, but sinners to repentance.

Mark 2:17 (KJV)

Chapter Twelve
Renewed

After twelve years of being confined to a bed, I finally escaped early 2017. This physical body has failed me so many times I can't even count. I constantly fought my brain everyday trying to accomplish the tasks set before me. I tried to go out in the world and work like a "normal person" for three years. God may have walked me through every interview, but he also walked me through every failure. I knew the path I was leading was not the plan He designed for me. I do believe my previous position in a medical laboratory was destined to be the last. God knew what was in store for my future and I do not want to jeopardize His plans, again. As I'm sure you know how easy it is to slip away from your calling. I refuse to let the devil chain me to that bed anymore.

I am renewed by the body of Christ and affiliated by Redemptive Gifts.

"Having gifts that differ according to the grace given to us, let us use them: if prophecy, in proportion to our faith; if service, in our serving; the one who teaches, in his teaching; the one who exhorts, in his exhortation; the one who contributes, in generosity; the one who leads, with zeal; the one who does acts of mercy, with cheerfulness."

Romans 12:6-8 (ESV)

Before I made the awful decision to change the path God was leading me, I was doing well succeeding God's plans. Even more heart trenching; so were my boys. I was accomplishing everything I had ever hoped for. My path was reversed and everything in my life fell apart, once again. But now I have no other choice than to move ahead. Isaiah 43:18 (NIV) tells us to "Forget the former things; do not dwell on the past."

Whether pre-planned by evil or accidental by man, the traumas from my past never made me an example, they made me a victim. But now, God has made me a testimony. So, I'm surrendering to Him. This was His plan. I trust His plans because mine always fail without Him. James 4:7 (KJV) says to "Submit (surrender) yourselves therefore to God. Resist the devil and he will flee from you."

Sometimes I must pause and catch my breath or clear the negativity that often surrounds me before I can continue to write. Every single word I type can easily be misconstrued if I allow the symptoms of sickness to distract me. The days and nights when panic hits, I remember the loss in my life. I quickly change my mindset because every time I open my mouth and claim victory over illness and loss, I win. I win because I have faith in the word that claims, by faith, I am a child of Abraham. (See Galatians 3:7 ESV).

 For years I have watched people from my church become miraculously healed. An instant burst of faith that meets God's expectations. I have experienced this great faith and I'm finally taking hold of it again. I've covered the walls in my room with scriptures. Fifty sheets of paper with scriptures taped to my wall might not look elegant but I'm pretty sure God's pleased with my devotion… and it's working. I rely on these scriptures. I see them every morning when I wake up. I'm surrounded by the word. Absorbing the word is what gives me the strength to open my mouth and claim freedom from oppression. I rely on the word for hope. (See Jeremiah 29:11 ESV).

I know that right now I feel well enough to write because I turned to the word instead of allowing myself to fall apart. I'm succeeding in His plan. I find hope and confidence in His promise that "I can do all things through Christ who strengthens me." Philippians 4:13 (KJV). But to receive this strength I must shut my mouth to negativity and claim the word of God over every obstacle in my life. I open my mouth when I have no strength, and I say His name. The name above all names, Jesus, Jesus, Jesus.

Everything is in the power of His Name. John 14:14 (ESV) says "If you ask me anything in my name, I will do it." Everything is in the power of the tongue. Proverbs 18:21 (DBY) says "Death and life are in the power of the tongue, and they that love it shall eat the fruit thereof."

By using the tongue for praise or evil, comes the fruit of it either good or bad. Well, I've swallowed that "fruit" for well over 12 years and I'm finally cleansing my mouth of the taste. Matthew 12:37 (NIV), says, "For by your words you will be acquitted, and by your words you will be condemned." I condemned myself for 12 years. If you're following in my footsteps, you are condemned as well. But don't worry, all you need to do is stop, and become hungry for the word. I did and now I am. I've dealt with many ladders in my life. After finding strength in the Word, I'm finally reaching the top. If I slip, faith always carries me back. Faith and knowledge in the Word are always there to rescue us. But when we speak the word, it becomes our greatest weapon.

I do believe God intercedes in our lives. Hebrews 7:25 (ESV) tells us that "Consequently, He is able to save to the uttermost those who draw near to God through him, since he always lives to make intercession for them." The Lord either leads me to help someone or someone is led to help me. I've had many opportunities to bring lost souls to the light. I have shared the love of God with many people. But until my knowledge of the word grew stronger, I was unable to convince them. I decided to educate myself in the word because Jesus says in John 7:38 (AMP), "He who believes in Me [who cleaves to and trust in and relies on Me] as the Scripture has said, from his innermost being shall flow [continuously] springs and rivers of living water". Also Mark 16:15 (KJV), that says, "And he said unto them, go ye into all the world, and preach the gospel to every creature." I am sharing the word to save you because the word is what saved me. I live in the Word and the Word lives in me. Without this knowledge, I would have no faith in the healing power of God, and I would have perished years ago. I would have burned in hell without any knowledge as to how to get out.

While bedridden, alone and weak, I never considered that someone else could be suffering as much as me. That's because I was never surrounded by anyone who was. For twelve years I only saw myself and I was the only person I felt sorry for. I had no one who could empathize and all I ever received was sympathy. I was consumed in my own trials and unaware of anyone else's. Then one day, God opened my eyes to see that someone else was suffering…. just like me.

The gift of mercy was instantly laid upon me while I wept with sympathy pain. I had experienced this pain before but had no idea it was a gift. I could feel her pain. It was agonizing as I rolled around in bed for hours each day. After experiencing her pain for only a few days, God showed her mine. We help each other get through the storms that fail to destroy us. But when there is nothing more that we can do for each other, we pray.

I never thought I would find someone who also suffered from chronic fatigue. We can empathize with each other and strengthen each other through our united faith in Christ. After praying with and for her, instead of myself, I have witnessed a traumatic shift in my life, for the better. We had both lived in bondage for over 20 years but through fellowship, we have broken our shackles and chains. I am more than thankful for you Lori, my united sister in Christ, and faith filled friend. "For where two or three are gathered together in My name, I am there in their midst." Matthew 18:20 (KJV).

God often reminds me of the famous story of Jesus Christ miraculously healing a woman with the issue of blood. In Matthew 9:20-21, Matthew, one of the first of His twelve apostles to observe the things of Christ, writes, "Just then a woman who had been subject to bleeding for twelve years came up behind him and touched the edge of his cloak. She said to herself, "if I only touch his cloak, I will be healed."

According to the book of Mark, this incident occurred while Jesus was traveling to Jairus's house, to raise his daughter from her death bed, amid a large crowd. A woman was there who had been subject to bleeding for twelve years. She had suffered a great deal under the care of many doctors and had spent all she had, yet instead of getting better she grew worse. When she heard about Jesus from Jesse, the brother of the apostle Simon the Zealot; who Jesus had healed from 28 years of paralysis at the Pool of Bethesda; her faith was abundant to believe that all she had to do to receive healing was to touch His garment.

Mark 5:29 grips me on a soul level when it says, "… she felt in her body that she was freed from her suffering." In my case, the word "suffering" is as sharp as a double-edged sword. It pierces my heart because I truly understand the meaning of that word. I've felt it, I've lived it and just like this woman, spoken about in three Gospel reports; Matthew, Mark and Luke, with Faith, I endured it.

Immediately after touching His cloak, Jesus felt the power come out of Him and asked, "who touched me". Jesus said in Luke 8:46 (NIV), "someone touched me: I know that power has gone from me." Seeing she could not go unnoticed, she fell at his feet and in the presence of all the people, she told why she touched Him and how she had been instantly healed."

Jesus explained how she had blessed Him with her faithfulness and said to her in Luke 8:48 (NIV), "…Daughter, your faith has healed you…"

I recall Luke 8:48 when I look back at the paths that led me to this day. Though I still remember the darkness, weakness and hopelessness, my greatest memory of it all, was the day my torment ended, and my testimony began. As I was struggling to carry myself, one day at church, my pastor, John Cappetto, stopped and asked me, "Tori, is that sho rt for anything"? I sighed in exhaustion and replied, "yes, Victoria". He looked into my eyes and said, "You are Victorious".

Throughout every obstacle I've faced in life, I have confidence in God that His biggest desire is that I am well. (Numbers 23:19 NIV). I declare I am healed.

Having the word of God to stand on, and each story that relates to mine, has given me the knowledge, hope and faith to say, "This is the day the Lord has made, I will rejoice and be glad in it." (Psalms 118:24 KJV). This is the day I will forever say, I was *Meant for More.*

Scriptures that Saved Me

Mark 11:23-24 (ESV)
Truly, I say to you, whoever says to this mountain, 'Be taken up and thrown into the sea,' and does not doubt in his heart, but believes that what he says will come to pass, it will be done for him. Therefore I tell you, whatever you ask in prayer, believe that you have received it, and it will be yours.

1 Peter 5:8 (ESV)
Be sober-minded; be watchful. Your adversary the devil prowls around like a roaring lion, seeking someone to devour.

Proverbs 15:2 (ESV)
The tongue of the wise commend knowledge, but the mouth of fools pour out folly.

Proverbs 3:5-6 (ESV)
Trust in the Lord with all your heard, and do not lean on your own understanding. In all your ways acknowledge him, and he will make straight your paths.

1 John 4:16 (ESV)
So we have come to know and to believe the love that God has for us. God is love, and whoever abides in love abides in God, and God abides in him.

1 John 1:7 (ESV)
But if we walk in the light, as he is in the light, we have fellowship with one another, and the blood of Jesus his Son cleanses us from all sin.

Romans 13:12 (ESV)
The night is far gone; the day is at hand. So then let us cast off the works of darkness and put on the armor of light.

2 Corinthians 11:3 (ESV)
But I am afraid that as the serpent deceived Eve by his cunning, your thoughts will be led astray from a sincere and pure devotion to Christ.

Luke 10:19 (ESV)
Behold, I have given you authority to tread on serpents and scorpions, and over all the power of the enemy, and nothing shall hurt you.

Isaiah 41:10 (ESV)
Fear not, for I am with you; be not dismayed, for I am your God; I will strengthen you, I will help you, I will uphold you with my righteous right hand.

Hosea 4:6 (ESV)
My people are destroyed for lack of knowledge; because you have rejected knowledge, I reject you from being a priest to me ...

Exodus 23:25 (ESV)
You shall serve the Lord your God, and he will bless your bread and your water, and I will take sickness away from among you.

Proverbs 2:6 (ESV)
For the Lord gives wisdom; from his mouth come knowledge and understanding;

Psalms 23:4 (ESV)
Even though I walk through the valley of the shadow of death, I will fear no evil, for you are with me; your rod and your staff, they comfort me.

Proverbs 18:21 (ESV)
Death and life are in the power of the tongue, and those who love it will eat its fruits.

Psalms 34:19 (ESV)
Many are the afflictions of the righteousness, but the Lord delivers him out of them all.

Proverbs 17:22 (ESV)
A joyful heart is good medicine, but a crushed spirit dies up the bones.

James 4:12 (ESV)
There is only one lawgiver and judge, he who is able to save and to destroy. But who are you to judge your neighbor?

Hebrews 11:1 (ISV)
Now faith is the assurance that what we hope for will come about and the certainty that what we cannot see exists.

Romans 10:17 (NKJV)
So then faith comes by hearing, and hearing by the word of God.

2 Corinthians 11:14 (ESV)
...even Satan disguises himself as an angel of light.

John 16:33 (NIV)
"I have told you these things, so that in me you may have peace. In this world you will have trouble. But take heart! I have overcome the world."

Isaiah 26:3 (DBY)
Thou wilt keep in perfect peace the mind stayed [on thee], for he confideth in thee.

2 Chronicles 32:8 (NIV)
With him is only the arm of flesh, but with us is the Lord our God to help us and to fight our battles....

2 Corinthians 4:4 (NLT)
Satan, who is the god of this world, has blinded the minds of those who don't believe. They are unable to see the glorious light of the Good News. They don't understand this message about the glory of Christ, who is the exact likeness of God.

John 3:16 (ESV)
"For God so loved the world, that he gave his only Son, the whoever believes in him should not perish but have eternal life."

Hebrews 9:27 (NIV)
Just as people are destined to die once, and after that to face judgement…

1 Timothy 4:10 (NIV)
That is why we labor and strive, because we have put our hope in the living God, who is the Savior of all people, and especially of those who believe.

Jeremiah 32:27 (NLT)
"I am the Lord, the God of all the people of the world. Is anything too hard for me?

Matthew 6:33 (ESV)
But seek first the kingdom of God and his righteousness, and all these things will be added to you.

1 John 5:14 (NIV)
This is the confidence we have in approaching God: that if we ask anything according to his will, he hears us.

James 1:6 (ESV)
But let him ask in faith, with no doubting, for the one who doubts is like a wave of the sea that is driven and tossed by the wind.

Proverbs 3:5-8 (ESV)
Trust in the Lord with all your heart, and do not lean on your own understanding, In all your ways acknowledge him, and he will make straight your paths. Be not wise in your own eyes; fear the Lord, and turn away from evil. It will be hearing to your flesh and refreshment to your bones.

Joshua 1:8 (KJV)
This book of the law shall not depart out of thy mouth; but you shalt mediate therein day and night, that thou mayest observe to do according to all that is written therein: for then thou shalt make thy way prosperous, and then thou shalt have good success.

James 4:7 (NIV)
Submit yourselves, then to God. Resist the devil, and he will flee from you.

Luke 1:19 (KJV)
And the angel answering said unto him, I am Gabriel, that stand in the presence of God; and am sent to speak unto thee, and to shew thee these glad tidings.

Matthew 14:31 (NIV)
Immediately Jesus reached out his hand and caught him. "You of little faith," he said, "why did you doubt?"

Mark 8:23-25 (AMP)
Taking the blind man by the hand, He led him out of the village; and after spitting on his eyes and laying His hands on him, He asked him, "Do you see anything?" And he looked up and said "I see people, but [they look] like trees, walking around." Then again Jesus laid His hands on his eyes; and the man stared intently and [his sight] was [completely] restored, and he began to see everything clearly.

Revelation 1:17 (GNT)
When I saw him, I fell down at his feet like a dead man. He placed his right hand on me and said, "Don't be afraid! I am the first and the last."

Romans 4:3 (NKJV)
For what does the scripture say? "Abraham believed God, and it was accounted to him for righteousness."

Matthew 6:14-15 (NIV)
For if you forgive other people when they sin against you, your heavenly Father will also forgive you. But if you do not forgive others their sins, your Father will not forgive your sins.

Mark 11:25 (ESV)
And whenever you stand praying, forgive, if you have anything against anyone, so that your Father also who is in heaven may forgive you your trespasses.

Luke 6:37 (ESV)
"Judge not, and you will not be judged; condemn not, and you will not be condemned; forgive, and you will be forgiven;

Colossians 3:13 (ESV)
..bearing with one another and , if one has a complaint against another, forgiving each other; as the Lord has forgiven you, so you also must forgive.

Numbers 14:18 (ESV)
The Lord is slow to anger and abounding in steadfast love, forgiving iniquity and transgression, but he will by no means clear the guilty…

Numbers 15:28 (ESV)
"If one person sins unintentionally, he shallower a female goat a year old for a sin offering.

Mark 3:15 (ESV)
…have authority to cast out demons.

Colossians 3:14 (ESV)
And about all these put on love, which binds everything together in perfect harmony.

Ephesians 4:32 (ESV)
Be kind to one another, tenderhearted, forgiving one another, as God in Christ forgave you.

Isaiah 43:1 (GNT)
…."Do not be afraid-I will save you. I have called you by name-you are mine

Job 36:12 (NIV)
But if they do not listen, they will perish by the sword and die without knowledge.

Proverbs 10:21 (NIV)
The life of the righteous nourish many, but fools die for lack of sense.

Colossians 1:17 (KJV)
And he is before all things, and by him all things consist.

Luke 10:19 (AMP)
Listen carefully: I have given you authority [that you now possess] to tread on serpents and scorpions, and [the ability to exercise authority] over all the power of the enemy (Satan); and nothing will [in any way] harm you.

Ephesians 6:12-18 (NIV)
For our struggle is not against flesh and blood, but against the rulers, against the authorities, against the powers of this dark world and against the spiritual forces of evil in the heavenly realms. Therefore put on the full armor of God, so that when the day of evil comes, you may be able to stand your ground, and after you have done everyone, to stand. Stand firm then, with the belt of truth buckled around your waist, with the breastplate of righteousness in place, and with you feet fitted with the readiness that comes from the gospel of peace. In addition to all this, take up the shield of faith, with which you can extinguish all the flaming arrows of the evil one. Take the helmet of salvation and the sword of the Spirit, which is the word of God. And pray in the Spirit on all occasions with all kinds of prayers and requests. With this in mind, be alert and always keep on praying for all the Lord's people.

Psalms 145:15-17 (GWT)
The eyes of all look to you, and you give them their food ant the proper time. You open your hand and satisfy the desires of every living thing. The Lord is righteous in all his ways and faithful in all he does.

Romans 12:6-8 (ESV)
Having gifts that differ according to the grace given to us, let us use them: if prophecy, in proportion to our faith; if service, in our serving; the one who teaches, in his teaching; the one who exhorts, in his exhortation; the one who contributes, in generosity; the one who leads, with zeal; the one who does acts of mercy, with cheerfulness.

Romans 5:8-11 (AMP)
But God clearly shows and proves His own love for us, by the fact that while we were still sinners, Christ died for us. Therefore, since we have now been justified [declared free of the guilt of sin] by His blood, [how much more certain is it that] we will be saved from the wrath of God through Him. For if while we were enemies we were reconciled to God through the death of His Son, it is much more certain, having been reconciled, that we will be saved [from the consequences of sin] by His

life [that is, we will be saved because Christ lives today]. Not only that, but we also rejoice in God [rejoicing in His love and perfection] through our Lord Jesus Christ, through whom we have now received and enjoy our reconciliation [with God].

Ephesians 1:7 (ESV)
In him we have redemption through his blood, the forgiveness of our trespasses, according to the riches of his grace.

Ephesians 6:12 (KJV)
For we wrestle not against flesh and blood, but against principalities, against powers, against the rulers of the darkness of this world, against spiritual wickedness in high places.

Jeremiah 29:11 (ESV)
I say this because I know the plans that I have for you." This message is from the Lord. "I have good plans for you. I don't plan to hurt you. I plan to give you hope and a good future.

Luke 19:10 (NIV)
For the Son of Man came to seek and to save the lost."

2 Corinthians 12:8-9 (NIV)
Three times I pleaded with the Lord to take it away from me. But he said to me, "My grace is sufficient for you, fo ray power is. made perfect in weakness." Therefore I will boast all the more gladly about my weaknesses, so that Christ's power may rest on me.

Proverbs 3:5 (ESV)
Trust in the Lord with all your heart, and do not lean on your own understanding.

Isaiah 40:31 (ESV)
..but they who wait for the Lord shall renew their strength; they shall mount up with wings like eagles; they shall run and not be weary; they shall walk and not faint.

Psalms 103:20 (ESV)
Bless the Lord, O you his angels, you mighty ones who do his word, obeying the voice of his word!

Isaiah 53:5 (NKJV)
But he was wounded for our transgressions, He was bruised for our iniquities; The chastisement for our peace was upon Him, And by His stripes were are healed.

Philippians 4:13 (KJV)
I can do all things through Christ who strengthens me.

1 Timothy 1:7 (NKJV)
...desiring to be teachers of the law, understanding neither what they say nor the things which they affirm.

Exodus 14:14 (ESV)
The Lord will fight for you, and you have only to be silent."

2 Peter 1:3 (NIV)
His divine power has given us everything we need for a godly life through our knowledge of him who called us by his own glory and goodness.

Isaiah 43:18 (NIV)
"Forget the former things; do not dwell on the past.

James 4:7 (KJV)
Submit yourselves therefore to God. Resist the devil, and he will flee from you.

Galatians 3:7 (AMP)
So understand that its is the people who live by faith [with confidence in the power and goodness of God] who are [the true] sons of Abraham.

Proverbs 18:21 (DBY)
Death and life are in the power of the tongue, and they that love it shall eat the fruit thereof.

Matthew 12:37 (NIV)
For by your words you will be acquitted, and by your words you will be condemned."

Hebrews 7:25 (ESV)
Consequently, he is able to save to the uttermost those who draw near to God through him, since he always lives to make intercession for them.

John 7:38 (AMP)
He who believes in Me [who adheres to, trusts in, and relies on Me], as the Scripture has said, 'From his innermost being will flow continually rivers of living water.'

Mark 16:15 (KJV)
And he said unto them, Go ye into all the world, and preach the gospel to every creature.

Matthew 18:20 (KJV)
For where two or three are gathered together in my name, there am I in the midst of them.

Numbers 23:19 (NIV)
God is not human, that he should lie, not a human being, that he should change his mind. Does he speak and then not act? Does he promise and not fulfill?

Psalms 118:24 (KJV)
This is the day which the Lord hath made; we will rejoice and be glad in it.

Tori has been a member of our church for many years. We have seen her grow in her faith tremendously over the years. Her testimony of healing is nothing short of a miracle of the Lord. We have watched her grow in faith, grow in her manifested healing and grow in her love for the things of God. Her testimony will inspire many.

Pastor John & Carla Cappetto

"Everything is possible for the person who has Faith."
Mark 9:23 (GNT)

I know it in my heart, and I feel it in my soul. Every word I've spoken and every obstacle I've faced was written to tell a testimony…and I've struggled and fought for twenty-seven years to share it with you. Twelve years of my life were stolen from me as I lay bedridden and ill and too weak to remember a day. Tormented by demons but too ignorant to claim my authority over them. I've seen the pits of hell and escaped through the heavens. I've fallen short of His glory and reached the highest steps. I've cried for my shepherd and met Him in space. He showed me His favor and made my paths straight. I've found victory through Faith—A Victory meant for us all. He broke my every chain and gave me the life He died for. From an honor student to a victim of a drunk driver, mother of triplets and bedridden and ill for over twelve years because I chose not to abort them… This is my Testimony of Faith.

About the Author

From those who know her, Victoria (Tori) Belcastro-Ray is a diversified writer of script, lyrics and poetry. After years of studying the word, and attending Rhema Bible College, Tori has graduated, a Minister of God. As the victim of a drunk driver, she has struggled and fought for 27 years, bedridden and ill, to tell her story. This inspiring testimony, influenced by the teachings of Kenneth E. Hagin, was written to encourage you that by faith, you too can receive healing from any ailment in your life. By reading this miraculous story, you will learn the scriptures Tori has stood on and the steps she has taken, to hold on to the Word of Faith.